For Instance, Sweetheart

For Instance, Sweetheart

Forty Years of Love Songs (1970–2010)

Written by Kawano Yūko and Nagata Kazuhiro

Translated by Amelia Fielden

For Instance, Sweetheart: Forty Years of Love Songs (1970–2010)
ISBN 978 1 76041 307 1
Copyright © text Kawano Yūko and Nagata Kazuhiro 2017
Copyright © translations Amelia Fielden 2017
Cover image: Nagata Jun
Proofreading: Marilyn Humbert

First published 2017 by
GINNINDERRA PRESS
PO Box 3461 Port Adelaide 5015 Australia
www.ginninderrapress.com.au

Contents

Translator's Introduction	7
Preface First of All	11
1 From Meeting To Marriage and the Birth of Our Children	25
2 Our Days As Youthful Father and Mother	43
3 America, From the Windows of the Green House	63
4 In Our Frantically Busy Daily Life	77
5 The Onset of Illness	103
6 Cancer Reappears	137
7 Last Writings: The Time That Was Left	157
Afterword	179
Appendix	180

Translator's Introduction

I feel greatly privileged to have been permitted to translate this remarkable book, their love story in poetry and prose, written by two remarkable people.

My first meeting with the most outstanding and prolific of post-war female Japanese poets, and author of more than twenty books, Kawano Yūko and her brilliant scientist/poet husband Nagata Kazuhiro were at their home in Kyoto in October 1999. Yūko had invited me there to discuss my proposed translation of her 1995 tanka collection, *Saigetsu*, *Time Passes*.

So began my happy years as Yūko's official translator and, I like to think, friend in poetry.

*

Yellow Balloons*

The first time I meet the poet, I am surprised to see how tiny she is.

A huge creativity married to a sprite-like physicality.

In her tanka and in our conversations over the following ten years, Yūko talks to me of her favourite things: feathers and plum blossoms; babies and daffodils; blue autumn air; cosmos flowers and balloons, especially bright yellow ones.

Yūko loves everything light.

Eventually the cancer thins her to a little voice in a fragile husk.

> a sunset cloud
> drifting
> beyond the horizon

*

* from *Mint Tea From a Copper Pot & other tanka tales* by Amelia Fielden, 2013

7

I admired Yūko immensely, and the effort of translating six books of her poetry, hitherto unknown to English readers, was absolutely a labour of love

Over the all-too-short time we shared, Yūko and I met in Japan at least once or twice a year between 1999 and her demise in August 2010.

On those occasions we variously worked on my translations, appeared together on NHK TV *Tanka Forum* programs, gave presentations at seminars, and participated in the Tower Tanka Society's monthly workshops.

I miss Yūko greatly, and reading the material in *For Instance, Sweetheart* has often moved me to tears.

Having said that, I should emphasise that there is much joy in the poetry and prose of this book, as well as the inevitable sorrow in its latter parts.

As a personal tribute, I offer here the following piece that I wrote shortly after the news came to me of Yūko's passing:

Time Passes*

Nagatani…
my eager mind, my fond heart
no longer seek
the way to the house
by the bamboo grove

*

'What do you want with my wife's work?'

'I want to translate it.'

'Can you do that?'

'Yes, I can.'

And so began my journey with a fascinating companion and no defined destination.

Of our first stage, collaborating on her 1995 tanka collection, *Time Passes,* Kawano Yuko (1946–2010) wrote this:

* published in *Mint Tea From a Copper Pot & other tanka tales* by Amelia Fielden, 2013

lifting her eyes	one by one
which had been fixed	my words are transformed
on my third tanka,	into English
she says 'ever'	with the gentle flexing
is better, more poetic	of her pencilled letters

Aside from ultimately translating six of her books, I was privileged to make two television programs with Yūko, and to participate in her Tower society's tanka workshops whenever I was in Kyoto at the right time.

Outside NHK studios, Tokyo   **a workshop at Kyoto University**

I wanted	fluttering
to say how much I	her Kyoto fan
admire her,	she glances
but we parted there	round the respectful room,
still talking of plum jam	sighs a sensei's sigh

Standing in her beloved cosmos garden as she farewelled me, eleven years after I had first journeyed to meet her, Yūko whispered 'Only a few more years, that's all I want…'

There were to be no more years, just a few more months.

though the grove
still rustles and talks
in her tanka,
the Nagatani Shrine gods
were deaf to her prayers

soon they will bloom
white pink mauve crimson –
the poet is gone
never to return home
to her cosmos garden

Amelia Fielden MA
Australia, 2016

Preface
First of All

On 12 August 2010, the life of Kawano Yūko came to a close. She was sixty-four years old. An unusually hot summer. And a day when the voices of cicadas seemed to drill into the heat.

My wife Yūko had been diagnosed with breast cancer in September 2000. After surgery she went into remission, but eventually a recurrence of the cancer was discovered in July 2008 and she lived for only another two years. When you think about it, she spent almost one-sixth of her life battling cancer; I could only pity her. And yet right through the long period of her battle with illness, up until the day before she died, Yūko kept on composing tanka poetry. I believe that it was writing tanka which gave Yūko the courage she needed to confront her disease.

We two came to know each other through tanka and then we married. Our first meeting was when Yūko was twenty-one and I was twenty. Both of us wrote a great deal of love poetry. Even after we were married, we kept on composing tanka addressed to each other as lovers and partners.

At the invitation of the Bungeishunju publishing company, I set about collecting our love songs and counting them again. Counting only the tanka which directly concerned our relationship, there were over 500 by Yūko and about 470 by me which could genuinely be called love songs.

Looking over them once more, I was surprised to find that not just during our courting days, but for almost all of our forty years together, we were writing like this. After Yūko's death, I wrote over a hundred more poems about her: tanka elegies, so to speak.

For publication in this book, *For Instance, Sweetheart*, I have selected 380 of the love songs we wrote to each other.

In addition to the tanka themselves, I have recorded, in each chapter, some of the prose Yūko wrote at various junctures, in order to familiarise the reader with the background to this poetry.

The third chapter of the book alone has none of my tanka, being composed solely of Yūko's poetry and prose, written during our stay in the United States when I was doing post-doctoral research at the National Institute of Health.

Whether in the beginning, the time of our early encounters, or at the end, Yūko's final days as a poet, I have written my words either as an involved party or as a bystander.

In Yūko's afterword to her first tanka collection, *Like a Forest, Like a Wild Beast*, there is the following passage:

> Encountering one certain person bound me inextricably to tanka poetry. Since then I have been composing love song after love song. There was a time when I tried to write just one such poem to my lover, but in the end was unable to. Tanka is definitely not something which one thinks of as being written for the sake of someone, or for some purpose. Tanka is more something intense, something more solitary, I feel.
>
> It is not for some person that I write tanka. That is even truer of my love songs. Rather, I believe they are allied to the grace and sincerity of my life as a woman.

That is the manifesto of one overflowing with youthful eagerness.

But of course she did not sustain this extremely proper stance on tanka composition as such.

In what way Yūko's eagerness might have changed with age possibly became clear to the poet herself, as she followed her tanka path.

For almost our entire forty-year period, we were writing from one to ten tanka about each other all the time. Really it was a strange scene. And in one sense I naturally feel shy about making it all public in this form.

However, on the other hand, it is true that there was a husband and wife couple who conveyed their feelings for each other through the medium of tanka poetry.

I do not think of love songs as belonging only to youth; writing in the tanka form lifelong should hopefully provide the opportunity of expressing such emotions.

Nagata Kazuhiro

Our Early Encounters

The first occasion when I met Kawano Yūko was a tanka gathering to organise publication of a journal called *The Fantasists*. The place was the Friendship Hall on the campus of Kyoto University.

It was 1966 when I entered university. The old-style senior high schools had already disappeared, but it was still a time of deep nostalgia for such schools. I myself had a strong yearning to be at the Number Three Senior High School rather than at Kyoto University. And it was a desire to wear the traditional Japanese male divided skirt called hakama that led me to the Aikidō (art of weaponless self-defence) club, as the first club I joined at university.

When I realised that only third-year students could don hakama, I gave up and quit the club after a couple of weeks.

During my five years at the university I wore wooden clogs almost all the time. I must have been longing for the out-moded roughness of the old-style senior high schools.

After that Aikidō club, I joined the basketball club. In junior high school I had played tennis ('soft tennis') from dawn till dusk. One could almost say I did nothing but play tennis. Even in matches in Kyoto city I did pretty well. But in senior high school I quit tennis altogether, and played around with basketball. I myself thought I was quite good. However, as might be expected, when I joined the university basketball club at the height of only 175 centimetres, I did not look like becoming one of the regular players. After practising receiving the ball until blood was coming out from all my finger nails, I gave that up before long, too. I was by nature athletic. And then, while I was dithering about the bother of joining a third sports club, I saw a poster advertising the inauguration of a Kyoto University Tanka Society. The autumn of the year I entered university, I joined this Tanka Society.

The Fantasists was a tanka journal put together by students from several universities in Kyoto. The core group comprised Kyoto University students and Ritsumeikan University students, with several students from Kyoto Women's University also participating. Yūko did not seem to belong to the Kyoto Women's University Tanka Society, but she was apparently invited by a more senior student in the Arts department to join in.

The day of our first Tanka Society get-together, I went into an upstairs room of the Friendship Hall (the Rakuyu Kaikan) of Kyoto University and there, standing by the window, was a young girl. I don't know what kind of hairstyle you'd call it, but most of her hair was tucked behind her ears on both sides, hanging down her back, with a layer of hair on top of it tied up with a ribbon. As I recall, she kept on with that same hair style for a really long time, after our marriage and even after the children were born.

Yūko herself wrote that I was the one who had got there first and was standing by the window (see Chapter 1), but my recollection is that she was there before me. We were there together for quite a while with a big, thick, wooden table between us.

When I showed her the journal of the Tower Society, which I had just joined, she evinced considerable interest in its cover. On the cover was a picture of dokudami herbs drawn by the artist Suda Kokuta. What I showed to Yūko was probably the July issue of the journal. (This too Yūko remembered differently.) From the time we started seeing each other, Yūko displayed an unusual amount of interest in plant life; in particular, she had a good knowledge of the names of even fairly insignificant wild flowers and grasses. It appeared that she was fond of dokudami herbs, too; taking the journal in her hand, she looked hard at the cover; then she must have read things inside, like the tanka which I had just begun to contribute.

Kawano Yūko had commenced composing tanka as early as junior high school. No doubt she was affected indirectly by her mother reading the tanka collections of poets like Nakajō Fumiko and Akashi Kaijin.

Perhaps Yūko was also influenced by her junior high school Japanese literature teacher, Sono Suzuko, who praised the tanka she had written. From the time she entered the senior high school attached to Kyoto Women's University, Yūko began composing tanka in earnest and submitting her work to various newspapers and magazines.

Tanka meetings are usually fora for submitting poems anonymously and having them critiqued by the members there. At such meetings, one learns the way of reading tanka; but, as one might expect, university student poetry gatherings are high-spirited affairs.

We students in the university tanka society were baptised by our leaders with avant-garde poetry and acted as if we were avant-garde ourselves; so we must have thought of the simplicity of tone in modern tanka as being 'old-fashioned'. It was a weird era, when impenetrability of meaning seemed to be highly valued.

Here is a tanka which Yūko produced on that first night:

> about to shake you
> suddenly I was
> truly saddened
> by your youth, and
> your so slender neck

It is a very straightforward tanka. However, no one understood the word maganashi in the third line. Even our leaders, the postgraduate students who had been doing tanka for years, shrugged.

Then, after waiting patiently for a while, Yūko ventured to ask, 'How come you don't get it? Maganashi is of course the word kanashi (sad) with the emphatic prefix ma in front of it.'

Nowadays that would be obvious, but such was the low level of the university students at the time...

Nonetheless, everyone was shocked that at an initial meeting, and amongst many who were older than herself, Yūko should express surprise at their lack of comprehension. Though she was quite nonchalant, there was not a skerrick of ill-will about her. At the same time, Yūko certainly gave me the impression that evening of being a rather sassy female. Looking back on it now, I can see this thought of her as a cheeky girl was indicative of the way I began showing my interest in her. Naturally I was also very conscious of the appeal to her of that young man with 'a slender neck' and I felt not a little jealous of him.

Several months after that meaningful inaugural meeting, *The Fantasists* was published. In November 1967 it appeared as *The Fantasists* Issue 0. A zero start-up! In this slim magazine of less than forty pages, I was secretly delighted to find Yūko's work printed after mine, I remember, so I guess she was already very much on my mind.

> the mysterious
> lovableness
> you possess –
> when you eat bread
> you look so young
>
> with all kinds of thoughts
> about Jesus
> who became a young man
> in the village of Nazareth,
> I closed St Matthew's Gospel
>
> Kawano Yūko, 'An Unripe Apple', *The Fantasists* Issue 0

I so desire	in slow motion
evidence of youth –	across the screen
leaving behind	gallop runners,
amaranths aflame,	their strained mouths
the town is darkening	disgorging summer

> Nagata Kazuhiro, Prelude • Summer, *The Fantasists* Issue 0

Side by side the difference in poetic skill between the two sets of tanka is self-evident, but at that stage Yūko already had about six years of tanka history behind her. It's natural there would be a gap between us. She knew how to lace her poems with candid expressions, but my amateur tanka were flung about with violent words.

Tsukamoto Kunio, who had been the standard bearer for avant-garde tanka in their peak period, kindly attended the meeting when we reviewed *The Fantasists* Issue 0. Carrying the weight of contemporary tanka on his shoulders, he was the poet who had the greatest influence on the young ones. Of course he was someone we could look up to; and the courteous way in which he critiqued the entirety of our coterie tanka was appreciated by us all equally. Probably Tsukamoto had no mean expectations of this group.

Personally, I was thoroughly delighted to be labelled by Tsukamoto Kunio as 'a splendid carriage horse'. However, these were of course not words of praise. I was pitilessly criticised for my work by everyone from Tsukamoto downwards. Yūko's *The Fantasists* Issue 0 is still around, and it has a huge number of comments on my work in it. Evidently she was beginning to be strongly aware of me, too.

The second time was a more personal encounter: we met up at a musical coffee shop called Ranburu on Higashiyama Street, near the Kumano shrine, where we were taken by senior students from our respective universities. I can remember the four of us having a long chat. After that, I don't remember how I came to see Yūko on her own. Probably the excuse was lending her a copy of the Tower journal.

So it went on, and we swiftly became close. Occasionally we would drop in to the coffee shop Ranburu. But when I think about it, at that time there were lots of cafés all over the city calling themselves musical coffee shops. Nowadays you'd be hard put to find one.

The second or third time we met, Yūko showed me a copy of *Waves*, the magazine of Kyoto Women's University Arts Department. Nineteen of her tanka appeared in it. More than those tanka, I was captivated by a piece of her work entitled 'Aster Flowers'. What she had in mind by showing me, I couldn't gauge, but to use a slang expression I was 'knocked out'. Now, rereading 'Aster Flowers', I see it as youthful writing obviously influenced by the literary style of Dazai Osamu and so on.

With the following abridged extract from 'Aster Flowers', I'll try to show you this, at the same time confessing to my own immaturity in being so readily enchanted by the writing.

> Although I believed for a long while that I had forgotten about him, when I sit like this at twilight on the veranda with aster flowers in bloom, feeling an extreme loneliness, I guess it is probably on account of that man…
>
> He has given me warm letters any number of times, but I've hesitated to reply; so finally he came calling at the melancholy time around the end of spring when the cherry blossoms had almost disappeared…
>
> That day I was feeling wretched, after one of my usual attacks had left me awfully dizzy and I was lying down in the tatami room with the rain shutters closed.
>
> My mother roused me, telling me a guest was here, but so listless was I, that I felt as if it were nothing to do with me.
>
> It was that guy I'd never met. Even though he was here, I still reacted this way. I was embarrassed to be caught sitting idly in a darkened room, and was considering how to escape. But when I thought of all the nice letters he had written to me, my attitude softened a little. I just combed my hair and, without putting on any lipstick, went out to the entrance hall.
>
> However, there was no one in the entry. As always, it was a tiny bit damp; there was just a smell of concrete floor. No trace of that guy anywhere.
>
> He wasn't there – and the fact that he wasn't there unexpectedly made me miss him a lot. I stepped down onto the concrete floor, opened the front door and had a look.
>
> Outside it was lightly clouded over, and because of the dusk, the air felt thin and insubstantial. That guy was standing near the hedge, swaying slightly. He had his back turned to me and was smoking a cigarette. When he became aware of me, he turned his torso around the way a branch bends and looked in my direction.
>
> The expression on his face was dim and lonely at the same time. The shade cast by the clouds suddenly cleared and there was a pink glow all around us. He seemed to be extremely embarrassed and stood there speechless, gazing into the dusk.
>
> Like that, without looking at my face, he said something in a low voice, as if to himself.
>
> 'Huh?' I replied; but like he hadn't heard anything at all, with strangely transparent eyes as if he were looking at a rare bird, he began to stare intently at my face. In that instant I felt everything around me go quiet.

I took the copy of *Waves* she handed me and went home. When I read 'Aster Flowers', I was clearly conscious of Yūko as my girlfriend. I wanted to wrest her from that young slender-necked guy.

Gradually the number of times we met, just the two of us, multiplied. It changed from once every few months to once a month, then to once a week, over quite a short period. When we couldn't bear seeing each other only once a week, it got to be two or three times a week. We met floating on a cloud of passion.

Just meeting made us happy. When we met, we would talk and talk, forgetful of time. We talked without reserve, ramblingly about everything: what we thought of tanka, things to do with our respective lives, the student movements which willy-nilly were encroaching on my environment, what the future held for me and so on. I always delighted in her merry laughter. We met; we walked and walked. We walked in circles, would perhaps be the way to describe it.

However, not long after we began meeting so frequently, I noticed more and more often a pained expression on her face. From little things she let slip, I got the feeling somehow that she might have some other boyfriend, who was pressing his suit. Maybe it was that young slender-necked guy I'd read about. I had begun seeing Yūko somewhat light-heartedly; and I had to process this possibility along with my now 'special feelings' towards her.

Amongst Yūko's tanka of this time was the following:

> gazing at the dark veins
> of leaves made transparent
> by the sun,
> I found myself in love
> with two men at once

By this time I was vaguely aware of the profile of that other man, but of course there was nothing I could do about the situation.

Kyoto Prefectural Botanic Gardens in midwinter. It was probably about a year since we had begun dating. In front of the frozen fountain, I kissed Yūko for the first time. We were under a great plane tree. There were few signs of other people in the winter gardens. I remember the feeling of the air around us: so empty, silent, and transparent you could see into the far distance. There was a large pond in front of the rose garden, and by the pond on one side, this tall plane tree. I think it is probably still there.

    I must have acted on impulse, but I don't have any recollection of the context. It was the first time I had ever kissed anybody. What I do remember is Yūko bursting into tears. And me, very upset, struck dumb, standing up straight in front of her. It must have been the conflict between her feelings for me and her feelings for that other fellow which brought on Yūko's tears.

>   ever bright there,
>   the sunset glow,
>   so I want
>   to reach the top
>   of that hilly path
>
>   for instance, sweetheart –
>   won't you sweep me off
>   as if
>   you are scooping up
>   an armful of fallen leaves
>
>   even when we
>   embraced passionately,
>   I was searching
>   for your heart
>   with my knife
>
>   for my sake
>   you were made into
>   a rose robber –
>   I was gazing up at you
>   as if you were a young lad

    Kawano Yūko, 'The Rose Robber', *The Fantasists* Issue 0

I am impressed afresh that one of Kawano Yūko's most famous tanka, 'for instance, sweetheart', appeared already in the first issue of *The Fantasists*. Yūko herself in later years reminisced that the composition of the first lines of 'for instance, sweetheart' had probably been influenced by the work of Tsukamoto Kunio, with whom she had become familiar through many encounters with him at tanka critiquing meetings. Yūko's experience of the vanguard poets came almost entirely from her participation in the gatherings centred on *The Fantasists*, and from tanka critiquing meetings held around that time.

Following our afternoon at the Botanic Gardens, I was delighted to see Yūko little by little inclining towards me as a person, in her tanka. I was relieved to feel the term 'sweetheart' had come to be used only for me. If I were asked about this, however, I could not readily affirm I was the 'sweetheart' of 'for instance, sweetheart'. One could say the same thing about the Rose Robber. In Yūko's lifetime I never asked her to confirm the subject of 'for instance, sweetheart' – and it was probably all right not to.

Although she seemed to be worrying a lot, Yūko was gradually showing a greater inclination for me. For all of her years, Yūko was a woman who never changed her whole-hearted way of living. The anguish of feeling that she was in love with two men at once, plus her mentality and her actual physical condition, appeared to be affecting her markedly.

While a senior high school student, Yūko had missed a year due to illness, and she was probably still suffering the after-effects of that. In our early encounters, she appeared bright and cheerful but she was actually quite fragile. Especially around the time we first met, Yūko was still lacking in self-confidence. Her withdrawal from high school and her hospitalisation cast a dark shadow, and even as a bystander I understood how painful this was for Yūko.

In the number 26 issue of *Waves*, to which I referred earlier, there is a set of nineteen tanka under the heading of 'Deep Inside of Me'. These are four of the tanka from that set:

> the loneliness
> of my enfeebled existence –
> without shadows
> from living things
> the sickroom window clouds
>
> crossing the path
> where mokusei flowers
> are scattered in an arc,
> my weary mother
> comes to visit me
>
> poor mother
> her hands so gently
> stroking my hair
> are sadly warm –
> I must get better
>
> even after the injection
> of anaesthetic,
> somewhere
> among my chilled nerves
> there is a slight pain

All of the above tanka were written while Yūko was hospitalised. I'd heard that she was in a hospital near Takatsuki, but she appeared not to want to tell me any more details, so I didn't ask.

From what she said in later years, it seemed like I had saved her by saying, at the time, that she was fine as she was. Nowadays I have no clear recollection of whether I'd said that kind of thing or not. What I can vividly remember is simply thinking that I must tether and attach to the world this frail person who seemed on the point of vanishing.

We are still dating. When our discussion touches on a delicate point, she suddenly says, 'You're going further and further away from me,' and faints. In coffee shops we usually sit with our chairs alongside of one another, and she falls forwards or sideways. I rush to pick her up, but the chairs are no good with her like that. Fortunately she weighs less than forty kilograms, so I can hold her in my arms. I carry her to the office to lie down. This was a repeated occurrence.

I was the total 'knight in shining armour'. It may seem somewhat affected, but the point was rather that I had to get her lying down, resting, with no time to lose. Although I was embarrassed at scooping up the almost-unconscious Yūko in my arms and carrying her off under everyone's gaze, I think there must have been a little bit of pride mixed in with the embarrassment.

At the time, I was living in the Iwakura district of Kyoto. She was living in Ishibe town in Shiga Prefecture. Inevitably our meetings went on until late at night. Mostly we parted at Kyoto railway station, but sometimes I escorted her back to Ishibe. We took the Tōkaidō line to Kusatsu, then changed to the Kusatsu line. Ishibe was the second station on the line. Yūko's home was about fifteen minutes' walk from the station.

Once, though, I knew if I took her all the way home, there would be no return train to Kyoto, I found it so difficult to tear myself away that I went with her anyway.

From Ishibe station on a bright moonlit-night along country roads. Depositing Yūko at her home, I watched her quietly and cautiously go in the back way; then I set off walking. By that time I'd seen her home on two or three occasions, and I had a good idea of the way. The last train had gone, so it would be a matter of walking back to Kyoto. What a stupid idea! But that's the sort of thing young people do. After taking Yūko home. I started bravely walking along the highway. Uh oh, it will take me till morning to get back to Kyoto!

What differed from my plan was the distance of the route. In addition, I was wearing wooden clogs. At night, lorries laden with goods thunder along the sides of Highway 1 at crazy speeds. The wind as they whoosh past is so cold. There were no pedestrian paths, so I was walking earnestly along the side of the road. In the fields on either side of Highway 1, the yellow wildflowers called tsukimisō seemed to go on and on forever. Every time a truck whizzed past, the flowers all swayed. And alongside those wildflowers a young man in wooden clogs was walking determinedly on and on. Looking back on that now, it is like a dream: a distant and a brave scenario.

Such were the patterns of our early courtship. But to get to the stage of marrying, we still had an incredibly long and complicated way to go. There is not room here to tell you all about that. When I think back to our courtship, I always remember how young I was that night of walking aimlessly on and on beside the fields of wildflowers.

1

'...the day I first heard
the sound of your blood'

From Meeting To Marriage
and the Birth of Our Children

'Although Nagata said nothing, I understood it all then.
Aah, this is such a lonely man.'

Timeline

1946   Kawano Yūko was born in Nanataki village, Mifunemachi, Kamimashikigun Kumamoto Prefecture, on the island of Kyushu.

1947   Nagata Kazuhiro was born in Aeba village, Takashimagun, Shiga Prefecture.

1951   Nagata's mother, Chizuko, died of tuberculosis.

1964   Kawano Yūko was absent from school in her third year of senior high, because of illness.
Kawano joined Miya Shūji's Cosmos tanka society.

1966   Kawano entered the Japanese Literature Department of Kyoto Women's University.
Nagata entered the Science Department of Kyoto University.

1967   Nagata joined Takayasu Kunio's Tower tanka society.
Nagata and Kawano met in July at a tanka meeting concerned with the first issue of the coterie journal *The Fantasists*.

1969   Kawano won the Fifteenth Kadokawa Prize for Tanka, for a sequence of tanka, 'Cherry Blossom Recollections'.

1971   Nagata was given employment by the Morinaga Milk Company and went to live in Kokubunji city, Tokyo.

1972   Marriage. They moved to Kikuna, in Yokohama city. Kawano published her first book-length collection of tanka, *Like a Forest, Like a Wild Beast*.

1973   August, the birth of a son, Jun.

1975   May, the birth of a daughter, Koh.
Nagata published his first tanka collection, *The Horizon of Möbius*.

for instance, sweetheart –
won't you sweep me off
as if
you are scooping up
an armful of fallen leaves

Kawano Yūko

wanting to meet
the me I was
before I met you,
I go swaying
on a bus to the sea

Nagata Kazuhiro

In 1967, as luck would have it, some Kyoto university students gathered together to produce a coterie journal called *The Fantasists*. The first meeting of the group was held in the Friendship Hall of Kyoto University. I seem to remember it was summertime. The Friendship Hall is on the campus of Kyoto University. It's a quaint old-style building, constructed in the late Taisho era. Apparently Nagata was the first to arrive for the meeting; he was standing by a window looking out. When I went into the room he turned around. I think that was the first time we met. We were seated on opposite sides of a table. He passed me a copy of the August issue of the *Tower* journal, with a picture of dokudami herbs, drawn by Suda Kokuta on the cover. On that occasion he apparently thought I was a bit cheeky. That was the impression I had of him too. So we both thought the other was cheeky [laughs].

When he was in senior year school, his Japanese teacher was a poet who belonged to the Araragi tanka society. Under that teacher's influence he wrote tanka and submitted them to the *Kyoto Newspaper*, where some were selected for publication as 'highly commended' poems. So he thought, 'I'm talented.' However, when he joined the Kyoto University Tanka Society and proffered the same tanka, I heard that they all appeared puzzled as to how to critique those tanka [laughs]. About six months later, a postgraduate student from the Medical Faculty, Fujishige Naohiko invited him to come to the society's meeting 'just one more time'. He went, and on that second occasion understood and appreciated, for the first time, what the others had to say. And then he was hooked.

[The next time we met] was at the coffee shop called Ranburu, near Kyoto University. I was taken there by Mifune Nagako, who was involved with 'new tanka'. I had a strong impression of him on that occasion: tall and slender, I thought he was really nice.

My family were in trade. I had the feeling that he must have grown up in an ordinary (middle-class) home. Actually his father was employed in a Nishijin sash wholesale store.

I once wrote about Nagata, 'He is like distilled water standing in a test tube.' That was really how he appeared: completely unworldly, though intelligent, and too delicate – so much so that I worried a little about his survival in society.

I too was fairly naïve, knowing little of the world, a bit of a coward, still unformed. Both of us were like that [laughs].

The distilled water and the well water came to live together in the end. That was us.

Kawano Yūko from People I Have Met

> peeling the bark
> from a camphor tree
> as I wait for you –
> this awkwardness too
> later I will recollect
>
> after slapping me
> on the cheek,
> you looked like
> you were about to
> break down and cry

'the dark sea
ebbing and flowing
full of blood' –
after our kiss we talked
of the maternal womb

    Kawano Yūko from *Like a Forest, Like a Wild Beast*

behind our backs
as we embraced, someone
breathing hard
ran by – and then
deep darkness

the Hydra constellation
trailing away to the south –
in the twilight
nothing said of loneliness,
we went our separate ways

elm trees
have elm tree sorrows –
when I think
of my blood unable
to dissolve in you

    Nagata Kazuhiro from *The Horizon of Möbius*

your hair
is tousled from sleep...
the wind blows it
when we walk along
a stretch of bright streets

> layered onto
> my recollection of cherry blossoms
> at twilight,
> is the day I first heard
> the sound of your blood
>
> calling me,
> such a young voice!
> his Adam's apple
> the size of a peach kernel,
> shining bright

> Kawano Yūko from *Like a Forest, Like a Wild Beast*

Cherry Blossoms

'This tanka is good. It is the best one you have written so far,' said my lover, in praise. My poetry had never been praised like that before. I was so happy.

Right, I'm going to write tanka, I thought. Writing, writing, writing, not just tens but hundreds of tanka; I'll keep on composing.

That tanka

> layered onto
> my recollection of cherry blossoms
> at twilight,
> is the day I first heard
> the sound of your blood

was a cherry blossom tanka. Just then, in the composite magazine called *Tanka* there was an advertisement calling for submissions for the Kadokawa Award for Tanka, with guidelines for submission and the judges' names. I, who was still a beginner as a tanka poet, had no idea of what kind of award, or how prestigious, this was. The descriptor 'unique gateway to the tanka world' was given. I didn't even know what that meant but I decided to submit some tanka to the competition.

For about a month, night and day, I busily composed tanka. Stockpiling tanka, I thought of nothing but poetry. My final university examinations were fast approaching, but study for them was the last thing on my mind.

I persevered with my tanka project right up to the deadline. The submission had to be postmarked the last day of February. I went and bought large sheets of manuscript paper and set about making clean copies of my work, but that took much longer than I had anticipated. Well after midnight and I still wasn't done. I felt warm and sweaty, short of breath; my head was on fire. When I opened the rain shutters of the living room, a breeze was blowing and snow was falling.

With the shutters open, I kept on writing and writing those clean copies. My fifty tanka were composed because of that one, all-important '...my recollections of cherry blossoms' tanka. Snow swirled in the wind. I wasn't even conscious of the cold. Using the whole of one piece of paper as a cover sheet, I wrote in the very middle of it 'Cherry Blossom Recollections'. Dawn broke as I finally finished my task.

Where were the cherry blossoms I wrote about, I wonder. For a long while I believed they were the cherry blossoms which bloomed in the cemetery at the Hōnen-in temple complex. In later years when I visited that place, however, the great old cherry trees which should have been there, were not. Perhaps I was mistaken. Perhaps they had withered with age. But I had the distinct impression that year, in the spring of 1968, the cemetery was full of blossoming cherry trees as far as the eye could see.

It was as if I were seeing nothing but cherry blossoms. Even when spring and summer were over, even when winter had come. So, then, that cherry blossom tanka came to me.

I had virtually forgotten about having submitted to the competition when, on 10 April, a telegram arrived from the Kadokawa Bookstore announcing that I had won. I was twenty-two, and the cherry blossoms were in their prime.

Kawano Yūko from *Kyoto* newspaper
18 March, Heisei 2, 1990

her hair, blown
into ripples like water –
one night
on the roof
closest to the sea

you – the sea –
kisses – and the sea…
I met with
beautiful words
on the night landing

her breasts seemed
as distant as the cape…
damn!
if only
I were older

trying
to return the sunset
to you there
beyond the fountain,
I am the grassland

anything unbalanced
is beautiful –
falling down
onto me, is the ocean
of your hair

      Nagata Kazuhiro from *The Horizon of Möbius*

when you approached me
breathing heavily,
I detected
in your eyes fire
like flaming arrows

my blouse
illuminated by the sun
of early summer…
within it, shimmering,
are my breasts

beside you,
sheltered by you,
I was glowing
like a gentle
bindweed flower

Kawano Yūko from *Like a Forest, Like a Wild Beast*

In the third grade of senior high, I suffered with my nervous system and took a year off school; I couldn't seem to recover from the after effects of that illness. It was a real problem for me, in that period, to get through one day at a time the way ordinary people do. Probably it was because of my over-sensitive nervous system, that the day after I walked through the congested area of Shijō Kawaramachi, I would end up spending in bed. When I strained my nerves even the slightest bit, I immediately became chilled through and had an attack of lethargy. I would eat almost nothing, as if I had anorexia. I had little realisation of being alive; nevertheless I was extremely sensitive and had no self-confidence towards anything.

That was the sort of state I was in when, through a tanka coterie, I began socialising with a certain young man. Little by little, this gave me more self-confidence in my life. I submitted my entry to the Kadokawa Award competition about a year after I started seeing him.

The real world irritated and pained my nervous system. Being introverted was the only way I knew to protect myself. One could say that it was through the membrane of my lover I was finally able to compromise and find a way of going on living in society.

Kawano Yūko, 'My Supports', *Contemporary Theories*,
February 1987

beginning
to understand you
a little,
less and less do I
understand men

knowing something
of your sphere
is both comforting
and lonely –
I peel a winter apple

don't die before me!
you bend to wipe
your naked body
that has more sheen
than new wood

you'll never
ever, have the smell
of a man –
your body has the scent
of new-mown grass

when you
approached me
smelling
of just-mown morning grass
my nipples stiffened

your lips
opened to start speaking,
are moist –
don't marry me
yet a while

Kawano Yūko from *Like a Forest, Like a Wild Beast*

> the lovely shadow
> of your chest — is that
> some sort of shape
> like 'giraffe grass'
> sticking out around it?
>
> Kawano Yūko from *Bindweed*

Nagata's proposal of marriage, at Kyoto Station, was made in these words: 'Won't you please wait a little while for me?'

Affected by the aftermath of student rebellions, his graduation from the university had been postponed for a year. That was the year when not even the entrance examinations for the University of Tokyo were conducted.

Around about the time we first started seeing each other, we had a date in Kurotani cemetery.

When I asked him, 'What kind of person is your mother?' he replied, 'She's got two eyes.'

With that, I burst into tears. Nagata has no recollection of having been held by his birth mother. He knows nothing at all about his biological mother. I had in fact asked about his second mother, his stepmother.

Although Nagata said nothing more, I understood everything then. He was such a lonely person. That phrase he used – 'She's got two eyes' – probably nothing more he could say.

Nagata is not someone to speak ill of others, but once or twice after that he said something negative about his stepmother, such as 'I grew up with my stepmother telling me she wished I didn't exist.' Kindergarten must have been a rather miserable time for him. It was about five kilometres from their house in Shichiku to Nishijin, where his father worked. But apparently Nagata had sometimes walked there to see him. 'It's a wonder I wasn't a delinquent when I was in senior high,' he told me too. He was certainly gloomy and lonely, though.

Those are not just my impressions. I heard from any number of people the comment 'Nagata has a shadow hanging over him.' This was my mother's impression of Nagata the first time she met him: 'Nagata has nice eyes, but there's a darkness about him.'

> Kawano Yūko from *People I Have Met*

as I held her
around the shoulders, she
struggled to stay upright
then came a toppling
I called 'tinted leaves'

making no attempt to move
in spite of
your drenched hair
your drenched shoulders –
you obstinate girl

a slice of lemon:
you
twirling it
like the firework
of a distant day

capriciously
I try lifting you,
in such a way
as to test the weight
of the fire within you

she chills
a little more swiftly
than the cherry blossoms –
evening comes to her
and then the darkness

the velocity
of her flying hair
is caught
by my chest, turned
into a deep blue horizon

slowly, quietly
she collapsed
hair first –
something like water
inside of my chest

    Nagata Kazuhiro from *The Horizon of Möbius*

in the deep hush
the voice of a cicada
sings on and on –
after giving birth
in dawn light I hear it

    Kawano Yūko

pregnant
in the hushed and dark
month of August
my wife tells me
she can hear cicadas

    Nagata Kazuhiro

The Maternity Hospital Cicadas

For me, who had just turned twenty when I wrote this tanka

> 'the dark sea
> ebbing and flowing
> full of blood' –
> after our kiss we talked
> of the maternal womb

the maternal womb was something I perceived as nebulous, still undifferentiated, a sea of blood before there was life in it. However, when I held in my arms a lover who had lost his mother as a young child, I was truly conscious of feeling, in a raw sense, the fertility of this womb I must possess, this sea of blood encompassing him too. Many times, along with my maternal instincts, I felt a kind of joy in restoring to him the time and place where his own life began.

> wistfully,
> in the womb-like darkness
> of foetuses
> kicking each other,
> we share embraces

In that tanka is described the period when encountering something in the darkness before birth, I prayed its body and soul would be a perfect whole.

When I was informed that I was pregnant, I was not all that happy. Morning sickness had already begun and I was overcome with total fatigue of mind and body. Yet when, late at night I crouched in the bath, sunk down to the bottom of the dark water, and closed my eyes, I considered with sorrow both my own body, now holding a life with which I must share my blood and flesh and bones, and that tiny life which was still only a piece of flesh. I thought of my own mother. Various images of my very young mother, pregnant with me and walking along under the rays of the summer sun, came surging into my mind like the sound of waves. Often I had the illusion that I was reliving my mother's time as a young woman.

As each day passed, I was conscious of the foetal movements inside me growing stronger; I felt distantly the sensation that I had been filled with a life not yet human. All sorts of thoughts floated through my mind: it was as if fish and plankton, and even more minute things, which existed before human beings, had swum upstream into our distant lifetimes, finally reaching the thick dark sea; and then, within the womb in my body had unerringly performed an act of creation. And thus the whole body becomes a sea, swallowing up anything and everything. On the other hand, the self can separate from one's own body and, without any sense of strangeness, go blending in with the full flood of life in our world.

For several days before the beginning of summer, when my mind was full to overflowing with the tide of such thoughts, I was walking around on the ground with a sense of expansiveness and abundance. My whole body was held steady, as if magnified by the earth, and life itself was dazzlingly bright.

I was admitted to the maternity hospital just after the middle of August. When I opened the window in my labour ward, I could see the white walls of the neighbouring temple. Along those white walls there were chestnut trees, paulownia trees, and a small garden. Even at noon the garden was shady. In the damp black earth were countless cicada holes; stuck to the trunks of the trees were numbers of transparent, toffee-coloured cicada shells. I could hear cicadas shrilling all day long like rain showers.

My labour pains began at twilight. While the pains were still slight, I stood by the window, gazing vacantly at the pale green shadows cast by fern fronds which flickered with light on the now darkening earth. They were not as noisy as they had been in the middle of the day, but I could still hear, faintly, the voices of cicadas like a ringing in my ears. Cicadas, the same as every summer; to me they seemed like dark creatures drilling into my soul. I was not able to stop thinking of the dark voices of those cicadas reaching the blackness in my womb, where the foetus must surely be listening to them. Then they were singing out the remainder of their inevitably short lives. I dreaded giving birth as I wondered at the strangeness of sharing this same period of time in which I myself was alive, with the foetus who still lingered in the darkness of the unborn. Inevitably, too, I thought of the form in which death might come at the end of this child's life.

With the onset of hard labour, I hardly opened my eyes until I gave birth. Perhaps it was instinctive to keep my eyes tightly shut in the face of this unknown experience. It was a hot night. The sheets were drenched with my perspiration. All I could do to stay decent, was try hard to suppress my moaning and groaning. I was virtually unaware of what was happening around me and who was saying what. And yet from dusk until evening and then into the night, like the distant tide, like a ringing in my ears, ceaselessly I went on hearing the cicadas

In intervals between the pains I would say to my mother at the bedside, 'The cicadas are singing.'

And she would respond, 'But the cicadas are not singing.'

What was I listening for with my ears, listening for with my heart, what was welling up and falling back all around me, was unmistakably the song of cicadas. It was like scores, no, hundreds of cicadas singing with all their might and main in the depths of a forest; it was like a great sound reverberating in my inner ears; still I could hear this strangely penetrating deep sound. Amidst hellish suffering, overwhelmed by my own groans, I continued to hear it; no, even now I don't understand why I was clinging to the sound of cicadas' voices. It was dawn when the baby was dragged from my body with forceps.

At that moment, too, I had my eyes tightly shut. Even when they finally brought the newborn child and laid him beside me, my eyes were closed. The day outside was greyish, shadowed like the bottom of water – and I could still hear the voices of cicadas. Yet there was not the enormous number of cicadas singing, like I had clung to in the midst of my labour pains: there was just one cicada voice singing on and on and on, with one shrill note.

Now, so many moons after that birth, I notice this tanka amongst those which I once composed as a girl:

> after the birth
> the mother is hearing
> deep in her ears
> the clear-toned shrill
> of a kanakana cicada

Once more I can't help thinking of the strangeness of this symbiosis between my mother and me.

There is also a tanka by Nagata, written around my second or third month of pregnancy:

> pregnant
> in the hushed and dark
> month of August
> my wife tells me
> she can hear cicadas

When I recollect that tanka, I can't help thinking back to my poem, 'after the birth'.

Kawano Yūko, Tanka journal, March 1974

> my heart full
> I soak in the night bath
> as in a spring,
> this body which now has
> two lives

> how tiny,
> how warm it will be –
> when summer comes
> I'll hold to my breast
> my own child

close to the lamp
I wiped dust from your eye –
unbidden came
the vivid realisation
'I am a wife'

only the child and I
know the feel of foetal movement –
outside of us
you as his father, already
on your lonesome

it was with fear
and trembling
that I touched
his naked body, too young
to be called 'father'

                              Kawano Yūko from *Bindweed*

2

'this nothing but this
is our family'

Our Days As Youthful Father and Mother

'frantically kicking out, hitting, embracing, pushing away, detesting him – in other words with my whole body I was questing, demanding something of the other person'

Timeline

1976   Kawano published her second tanka collection, *Bindweed*. Nagata resigned from the Morinaga Milk Company in Tokyo to undertake unpaid scientific research in the Chest Disease Research Institute at Kyoto University.

1977   Nagata published his second tanka collection, *Golden Section*. Kawano was awarded the Twenty-first Contemporary Poets' Association Prize for *Bindweed*.

1979   Nagata was awarded a PhD in Science from Kyoto University for his research on Differentiation of Mouse Myeloid Leukemia. He was appointed a lecturer at Kyoto University.

1980   Kawano published her third tanka collection, *The Cherry Blossom Forest*.

1981   Kawano was awarded the Fifth Contemporary Women Poets' Tanka Prize for *The Cherry Blossom Forest*.
Nagata published his third tanka collection, *The Infinite Trajectory*.

1983   The family moved to Ishibe, in Shiga Prefecture.

1984   Kawano published her fourth tanka collection, *The Spirited Male*.

did you just now
step over a small puddle?
the spoon
I am polishing
has clouded, by chance

                    Kawano Yūko

now,
with poverty dispelled,
the baby carriage
goes along under a hot sky
of cumulonimbus clouds

                    Nagata Kazuhiro

even now I love
the violence with which
you roughly
grab my shoulders
and turn me around

in the night-darkened room
pulling off your singlet
silently,
your shape from behind
is like a young giraffe

how sad for you
never to know your mother –
a crane grazes
at the distant water's edge
glowing in the setting sun

                  Kawano Yūko from *Bindweed*

hitting you
hitting the kids – oh,
my hand's on fire...
frantically loosening my hair
I go off to bed

is the child me
am I the child?
inseparable
child in my arms I bathe
child in my arms I sleep

>   Kawano Yūko from *The Cherry Blossom Forest*

I realise now that my way of child-rearing was somewhat of a shambles. At the time, we were living in a very small house right in the middle of a row of three Kyoto terraced houses. My husband had gone back to the university, and was working as an unpaid researcher – there was no remuneration, only the title of 'researcher'. To make a living, he was also teaching at an evening cram school, returning home every night very late. After he had eaten his meal, he would grind coffee beans with the mill held between his thighs, and then set to composing tanka and writing critiques. As for me, having been looking after the kids all day long, I was exhausted; but not to be outdone I too sat up to compose tanka, leaning against the kotatsu heater.

We were both really pushing it and had neither the time nor the strength to carry on like that. So, inevitably, we would quarrel. When we argued, the kids would wake up and start howling. Having said that, those children were my motivating power; I was unable to make a distinction between us. 'is the child me / am I the child?' Such a really short period that was, when the kids were young. And the period when I was so closely bonded with them, when they aroused the most explosive emotions in me, was also short. All in all we were desperate.

>   Kawano Yūko from *Commentaries on My Tanka*,
>   Bokusui Prize Winners' Series: Kawano Yūko

as in your youth
when you had no wife, no child
no occupation,
you still look powerless
and vulnerable

you cannot even tell a lie –
I'm looking up
at your hair
casting a shadow
as it flops over your forehead

obviously
I can't escape
from your strong hands
grasping my shoulders,
from the power of a man

even the poems
I've stayed up late
writing about you,
whom I love so fondly,
still all belong to me

those random lies
I so casually
told you,
they must really
have cut you to the quick

  Kawano Yūko from *The Cherry Blossom Forest*

night after night drinking
as if just to get drunk –
quite incidental
that I have children,
that I have a wife

her faint sleeping breath…
my wife has her own nights…
if I don't tell her,
no way she'll know
of my loneliness

'the loneliness
of face to face' –
be that as it may,
the evening sun quietly
fills the transparent vase

rain on the cape,
I might write –
on the days I don't see her
I go to bed
wearing my black sweater

I left the room
where we had argued –
in the deep noontide
the bird's eyelids
are closed sideways

    Nagata Kazuhiro from *Golden Section*

like a lizard
stuck fast
to a baking hot wall,
I was trembling –
how I hated him

though I hate him,
hate him bitterly, for now
I jump into the bath
submerging myself
up to my ears

from my willingly
rain-beaten hair
comes a smell –
I belong to no one,
not then, not now

after all
when I think about it
I don't know you
for whom I open the door
and wait every night

ah, your tenderness –
you are in my sight
I want your kisses
so much that
my whole body trembles

    Kawano Yūko from *The Cherry Blossom Forest*

without even
embracing her
I get a faint smell
of creosote
until I fall asleep

when I run my fingers
through her hair and hold her,
a distant scent
of grass arises
from her night hair

casual words,
but they came back to me
as I crossed
the watershed
of dawn darkness

    Nagata Kazuhiro from *Golden Section*

the scent of your body
smelled, that early summer
in the sparse wood –
how come you
still carry it?

you have
red eyes tonight
really red, those eyes,
and beside them
am I

those hands of yours
which possessed me
last night, so easily
drawing on white paper
a perpendicular line

my burning hatred
has swollen tonight –
not even an ant
which has lost its way,
dares brush against me

if I don't touch him,
he's just a man –
back-lit in the sunset
cicadas are singing,
annoying, irritating

last night
why was it
you hesitated –
that big hand dangles
over the back of a chair

Kawano Yūko from *The Spirited Male*

15 June 1979

Koh is crying and sleepless. She's got tonsillitis again. All through May, Jun and Koh took it in turns – twice each – to have fevers. I was helpless, just thinking, 'Not again.' I'm sick of this.

My head aches through lack of sleep. I've been to the dentist and had a molar nerve removed. He made an incision in my swollen gum. I came home feeling a bit worse. Finished reading *The Dark Journey* by Kurahayashi Yumiko. Jun has got feverish again in the night. Doesn't matter how much ice I make, it's not enough.

18 June

In the early afternoon, a phone call from Professor Yasuo Ishikawa at the laboratory. Apparently, Nagata had an accident doing one of his experiments. He said that Nagata caught it in the eyes when there was an explosion of the solid sodium hydroxide and undiluted sulphuric acid. After three hours at Kyoto University Hospital having his eyes treated, Nagata came home. Both of his eyes were bright red and bloodshot – they looked terrible. He also had burns here and there on his face, arms, and chest. His shirt was drenched in chemicals, and there were holes in his jeans, too. Drops had to be put in his eyes every five minutes. I was just relieved that was all of the damage. My parents called from Ishibe several times, anxious about him.

19 June

Nagata was appointed lecturer at Kyoto University, an informal appointment. When the kids were asleep, we opened a bottle of champagne and celebrated, just the two of us. It's two and a half years since he returned to Kyoto (as an unsalaried researcher). He's been working day and night ever since; it's been a 'back to the wall' existence for us.

Nagata has been wearing three hats: doing his scientific research, teaching at the cram school to make ends meet, and writing literary manuscripts, while I looked on from the sidelines nervously all the time. With his university appointment, finally, we could draw a line under that life. My husband has achieved real success here, taking his doctoral degree and obtaining a lectureship. As for me – what on earth have I done since returning to Kyoto? After we finished the champagne, we opened some beer. While we were chatting about this and that, it got to half past three in the morning.

Kawano Yūko from 'A Poet's Diary',
Tanka Gendai, August 1979

> for a while, I was stroking
> the thick bushy eyebrows
> which have brought
> this spirited male
> into his thirties

> ah, the loneliness –
> beyond the lilies
> massed in a vase,
> beyond the crowd of people,
> you are there

> my better half
> displays the spirit
> of a modern student,
> with his long hair, long body
> clad in black shirt and jeans

Kawano Yūko from *The Spirited Male*

> together we fall asleep
> and I dream of dogwood blossom –
> should you ask me
> I'd want to respond
> 'this is gentleness'

the night when
utterly exhausted
we go to bed desolate,
a stray owl
is calling in the distance

a spring at night, water
welling on top of water –
when we embrace
our love is
unquestionable

        Nagata Kazuhiro from *The Infinite Trajectory*

as you stand waiting
there in the sunshine
your shadow
is like a barrier,
so long are your legs

holding
you two children
in my arms
I still have space to include
your father's emotions

        Kawano Yūko from *The Cherry Blossom Forest*

    The first thing he said after we were married was 'You and I were brought up quite differently.' I really thought so, too. This man was someone who had never been given unconditional love and, I realised, had always been lonely. I thought of him as a sort of doughnut, with nothing in the centre. Even now that's the feeling I have. If I die before him, I wonder what he'll do. Most likely he'll drink too much and get so drunk that he'll drown in the bath.

    Yes, I intended to love Nagata with all my heart. Although never poverty-stricken, his was a lonely childhood and adolescence, I was sure. His stepmother suffered from atrophy of the cerebellum, finally becoming virtually bedridden, so the three siblings had to take it in turn to prepare the household meals. Nagata's family was not a happy one. For that reason, he has valued our family all the more. All the love which he never received as a child, he has poured onto his own children. He has been a really good father.

Only once did I regret marrying Nagata. Aside from that time, I have had no regrets. That once was when we were living with his family and I was the 'daughter-in-law'. Jun was about to enter elementary school, and we were living with Nagata's father and my sister-in-law. As the 'daughter-in-law', I did my very best; however – maybe it was a case of 'horses for courses' – they didn't seem to take to me in spite of the efforts I made towards them. Probably a daughter-in-law who was always writing poetry and reading books was not very appealing to them.

One night, when Nagata and I were quarrelling, he (my father-in-law) came and said, 'Get back to Ishibe' (where my birth family lived). Holding the two small children in my arms, I was crying. I thought of the old saying 'There is no home for a woman in her three worlds.' This house where I was living – furniture and all – was cold as ice, I felt. I detest the expression 'daughter-in-law'; but if a 'daughter-in-law' has the ear and the support of her husband, she can put up with quite a lot. At the time I am speaking of, Nagata did not defend or protect me. That's something I'll remember all my life; it's a wound which won't heal.

At a stage in my life when I had absolutely no confidence in myself and going on living was almost unbearably painful, I had met Nagata. I was still not recovered from my nervous illness. And he told me at the time, 'You are fine as you are,' which was very reassuring. Until then I had been stumbling along, naked in my sensitivity. This person, Nagata Kazuhiro, was like a poultice wrapping around and easing my life.

Kawano Yūko from People I Have Met

see nothing
hear nothing
say nothing –
now my position is that
of a frozen daughter-in-law

though I raise my voice
frantically,
icicles hang
from this house where
everyone speaks in a whisper

leant against you
as the bus
swayed along
I was dozing,
then in my twenties

    Kawano Yūko from *The Spirited Male*

I've a vague recollection
of running my fingers
through my hair,
momentarily blown in the wind…
and you smiling

against my shoulders
you, resting asleep,
in your hair
salt from the sea
as it dried

sprinkling the garden
water gushing
in the afternoon
oh God, my sexual drive
like a giddy spiral

such a long time
until I can call my own
this woman
I'm holding against me –
rain beats on the windows

at a frenzied moment
the evening glow
is reflected
on her beautiful expression –
you belong to me

    Nagata Kazuhiro from *The Infinite Trajectory*

saying nothing
these dumb fireflies –
taunting me briskly,
like a sun shower,
this woman

I was told
you wanted to look at the world
through your own eyes…
the cherry blossom that night,
the colours of that lake

you were waiting there
in rain so heavy
your breasts were drenched –
we should abandon tomorrow
and even this moment now

at the last ditch
she smoothly casts off
all logic
and laughs in glee,
like a scatterbrain

though people say
you have given up hope
of getting some peace
and I agree,
wind ruffles the trees

when I feel them
from behind, oh God
her breasts made
just the right size
to fit in my hands

facing the opposite direction
she urinates,
making me wait
in the darkness
where yellow flowers sway

enmity
emanates from my wife
extends to the kids,
our kids, so to my wife
so to her husband…

        Nagata Kazuhiro from *The Arrow Cart*

I wonder if
that pendulum thing
does hang vertically –
I think of him
as a sharp, slender, man

through your words –
no,
through your hesitant voice
I am savouring
your doubtful heart

> I'm the audience
> for that man,
> Nagata Kazuhiro –
> it is quite fun
> observing him
>
> this, nothing but this
> is our family –
> the two kids
> in place between us
> we climb the hill path
>
> Kawano Yūko from The Spirited Male

'This, Nothing But This, Is Our Family'

Many years ago, when my elder child was still in my womb, I attended a meeting of a coterie of women poets who were involved with the journal *Tanka*. Suddenly, casually, I tossed off the comment, 'I am filled now with both life and death.' After I said it, I was surprised at myself. Words are strange things: they give expression to what is floating around vaguely in one's subconscious mind. It was like that then.

There was no need for me to use such 'big' words as life and death; and yet I had a strong sense of my unborn baby as a being who would exist only temporarily, for some non-specific period.

Compared to children, other people have more certainty about them; their outlines are clearer, as it were. Although I expected to know my children from the onset of their lives, although it was totally clear the moment my children were born would be the true start of my own life, it made me even more conscious of the transitory nature of children, perhaps.

The feeling of powerlessness that they were children I had born. It was the powerlessness I felt about my own existence. However, children are children. They were not my clones.

The wonder of being with them all the time, from the beginning of their lives, of watching them closely as they grew and matured. Nowadays I ponder again the mystery of growth, as I relive the times they went from suckling babies to infants, then from infants to children.

Much is said about the blood ties between mother and child, their indivisibility, that there can exist no tighter relationship. Yet, compared to the mysterious aura of transience which children bear, the existence of that complete stranger, my husband, feels more certain to me.

When my children were about two or three years old and I was watching them at play, I got the sense of life just beginning. I often thought about the isolation of the individual. They were too young to have a clear consciousness of self and other; the world surrounding them had no firm boundaries; they could just see only what was immediately around them. When I observed my children in this period, innocent as they were of that 'isolation of the individual', it seemed visible in them, to me.

> my child
> having drawn a great oval
> on white paper,
> enters the oval
> and plays by himself
>
> in those days when
> the child and I were one body,
> I did not realise
> I could lose sight of him
> even in the sunshine
>
> Kawano Yūko from *The Cherry Blossom Forest*

I don't place great emphasis on blood ties; but the consciousness that my children will live on after me probably comes from the fact that they are beings to whom I myself gave birth.

I come back home from a short trip, four or five days away. I meet up with the children I've left to be cared for by others for four or five days. And am surprised when I look at them. They seem like a stranger's children. They don't feel like my children any longer. They smell of 'otherness'; the sense of a different home envelops them. This feeling that they are not my children is something I always have after a trip away, even a short one.

To me a family is just parents and children; but even one's spouse must always be in some sense an incomprehensible 'other'. The 'family' which lives in one house and sits at one dining table comprises husband and wife, parents and children. Between husband and wife, in particular, are bonds which are frail and brittle, liable to break easily with just one word. I take this fragility very seriously; I very strongly prioritise and protect my marital relationship, these days. That's my position.

We perform variously the roles of father, mother, children; and yet none of us gets at all accustomed to our respective roles. Viewed in the light of family relationships as a whole, I guess that's only natural. Even now, I have difficulty conceiving my separate roles as mother, housewife, and spouse – let alone old lady.

For example, this tanka from *The Cherry Blossom Forest:*

> is the child me
> am I the child?
> inseparable
> child in my arms I bathe
> child in my arms I sleep

undoubtedly expresses the indivisibility of mother and child. But it can also be interpreted as a search for my own self – how much of this is me? I don't know what I am…

> after all
> when I think about it
> I don't know you
> for whom I open the door
> and wait every night

> Kawano Yūko from *The Cherry Blossom Forest*

what I know
is only one side of you –
right now
you're lazily eating ripe melon,
elbows on the table

ganging up,
three friends of my kids
call me
'old lady' – funny
to be an 'old lady'

Kawano Yūko from *The Spirited Male*

In *The Cherry Blossom Forest* and *The Spirited Male* I'm moving about a lot: frantically kicking out, hitting, clutching in an embrace, pushing away, hating him…in other words, I was probably reacting with my whole body to the 'otherness' in him.

I didn't understand myself, who I was, or who my partner was. I must have been carried away by that lack of understanding. But fundamentally I couldn't expect to be able to understand the other party, to understand what sort of a person this was. My poetry became a forum for asking such questions about ourselves; and it was also part of the process of asking the questions:

washing his hands,
gargling,
back to me
is a man
I can call my spouse

this person
long-legged, well-muscled…
each dark-as-leopard-flowers night
I look up at him
and cannot know him

Kawano Yūko from *The Spirited Male*

And then this tanka:

> this, nothing but this
> is our family –
> the two kids
> in place between us
> we climb the hill path

represents my family.

From here on too, I will continue composing tanka staying close and caring for this, my family.

Until now, even in my tanka, even in my day-to-day living, I have always been actively involved this way.

Little by little, my children are entering the realm of adulthood. Expending even more energy than he did in the period when he was an unsalaried researcher, my husband is forced to use each and every one of his days to the full. This is the prime of his life. The patterns of our family are continuing to change. I myself have no idea how things will go in the future amongst these 'others'.

Kawano Yūko, *Tanka*, March 1987

3

'what is wrong with being a good wife'

America, From the Windows of the Green House

'That, for Jun, was the best way of encouraging himself. While they were cloaked in cheerfulness, all of the letters he wrote represented SOS signals from him to his motherland, Japan.'

Timeline

1984 In May, Nagata went to America, having been invited to occupy the post of Associate Professor in the National Cancer Institute of the National Institute for Health.

In August, Kawano Yūko and their two children arrived in New York. The family then lived in Rockville, Maryland, for a while. In December, they moved from their apartment in Rockville to a small green detached house. They rented a truck and did all the work of the move themselves.

1985 Jun graduated from Japanese School. He joined an American football team; the whole family became hooked on football. From time to time they went camping on the Atlantic coast. Yūko's parents were invited over, and they went on a trip to near the Canadian border.

1986 Yūko's asthma worsened. In May, she travelled to the West Coast of USA and then back to Japan, to live in Ishibe again.

In October, Nagata was appointed Professor at Kyoto University (chest tuberculosis laboratory, cell chemistry section).

In November, Nagata assumed the editorship of the *Tower* journal. Yūko published a collection of essays called *From the Windows of the Green House*.

my son
back home after a beating,
keeps silent –
I will tell his father about it
without questioning Jun

has your youth
finally left you?
your reticence
now embellished
with a bristly beard

even in a dream
my temper explodes,
kicking my husband
with great force
I wake up

Kawano Yūko from *Koh*

SOS Signals

'For a start, the best guys get to be captains. Then the captains do scissors, paper, rock, and the one who wins, chooses the best players for his team, in order.'

'So, what number were you, Jun?'

'Half.'

'What?'

'Half – halfway. I'm chosen about seventh or eighth. This happens in Japanese school. In American school, I'll be able to make captain for sure. Only when I can speak English.'

When we had this discussion, I was really surprised, even a bit shocked. How stringent boys' society is, I thought. It sounded like a mini version of adult male society, to me.

'Yep, guys who are weak at sports are no good.' So said our son, who at home is untidy and extremely unreliable.

Talking of 'weak', every day Jun came home having had a quarrel with someone or other. It seems he hardly ever won these fights. Sometimes he even turned up with his face swollen.

'Who did you fight with today?'

'A negro guy, Misai. He gets mad straight away,' he said, forgetting all about his own frenzied habits.

No doubt this was something he got from me, his mother: being weak with just a strong will and quick to quarrel.

The boys he fought with were usually negroes or Koreans or Chinese – or so it seemed. There was also the affair of the white boy, Levi. Recently, when I went to an observation day at the school, I had a look at this Levi. Levi appeared to be a kid who couldn't follow the lessons.

That boy, Levi, came by our house one day with two of his henchmen, before Jun was back from school. These boys, much bigger than I, surrounded me and started shouting in unison, 'Today, at school, Jun hit us.' Or that's what I thought they were saying, and I didn't understand what they said after that. As soon as they saw Jun coming home, the three of them rushed up to him. Jun tossed aside his schoolbag and flew off somewhere.

'Heaven help negroes and Koreans!' Jun once uttered as if by chance. I wondered what he had witnessed at school that day.

Considering the matter carefully, I saw that the boys with whom Jun fought were only kids who were usually isolated from the other students in the class. Such kids probably targeted this Japanese newcomer who could not speak English. For Jun, these days of 'internal troubles, external woes', so to speak, continued. The pain of not speaking Japanese. His helplessness in English.

Jun wrote innumerable letters to the school he had previously attended in Japan. His letters were filled with only the positive aspects of life in America. He wrote with elation, as if he were having a good time.

Rather than showing off, this was Jun trying to give himself wholehearted encouragement. While they were cloaked in cheerfulness, all of these letters he wrote represented SOS signals from him to his motherland, Japan.

Summer passed, autumn passed, and the year end; no replies came from Japan.

'Why, why, don't the teachers or those guys answer my letters?' Jun was really angry, so angry that he gradually became unable to speak about this. He went beyond anger into a state of intense loneliness. Even so, he looked in the letter box again today.

Kawano Yūko from *From the Windows of the Green House*

> when you are grown up
> don't you forget
> your father
> playing chess with you
> after you'd been beaten at school
>
> an indigo night sky
> pounds against the shore –
> the father and son
> fishing off the beach,
> are still not back
>
> only twice
> does he use the flowery word
> 'darling' –
> phone conversations with him
> always short and simple

Kawano Yūko from *Koh*

A Parent As a Friend

At our local school (in Maryland), he had a fight; there was some sort of trouble between Jun and his young Japanese fellow students, and he came home hurt. Although I more or less knew what had happened, I stepped back a little and looked at him in silence.

Eleven years old. Almost pubescent. Jun, at the end of his childhood, needed his father.

His father came home, and the four of us sat together at the round table for dinner. Perhaps Jun would like to take a bath with his father. On these occasions, Jun would drop into the conversation some of the unpleasant things which had happened during the day, mixed in with the good and fun things. No one referred directly to it, but we all understood what was paining Jun the most.

The day he came home with his face swollen, Jun didn't say who had hit him. After we'd finished dinner, it was still light outside. Father and son were discussing something. Then they went out with a baseball and a glove. At such times, Jun's father gives the appearance of being carefree and having fun. Even when he came home sweating a bit, he seemed to have enjoyed himself. And his son came back looking as if all his worries had been swept away.

They took a bath together, then secluded themselves in the kids' room, and began playing Japanese chess on the bed. After a while, amidst Jun's yells I heard his father murmuring, 'I'm playing for you, without using all the chess pieces. Pull yourself together!' And something to the effect of 'Hey, don't you go buying into any more stupid quarrels.'

While they played numerous games, the father was amusing himself and it got very late into the night.

Then it was as always, 'Don't bother with your homework tonight.' This father only ever hit his son once or twice. I never saw him come down hard on Jun.

When Nagata was really small – not even five years old – his birth mother was taken from him; he spent a lonely childhood. That background is most likely why he wanted to cocoon his own son.

To the eyes of outsiders, he may have seemed like a very understanding, kind and gentle father, in this new-fashioned nuclear family. I, as an insider, did not think this. Sure, he was kind and gentle; but this gentleness of his was somehow of a different nature to that of the patriarchs of old who would watch over and protect their sons while keeping their distance.

He was neither close to his son, nor remote from him. He interacted with Jun by wearing jeans and playing catch with him – that was the sort of 'distance' between them. It was the distance of being able to see the other's whole body and feel the warmth of a hand on the ball. Standing on the same piece of ground as his son, he does not see his son from above his head.

At least this kind of father figure is not what our generation had as fathers.

In our students days over twenty years ago, he walked around in wooden geta clogs all year long. He wore jeans and geta, and clattered along, jeans swishing. Because of his long legs, he would drag his feet as he walked, so he didn't make a happy clopping sound. From his student days until now, he has maintained his bookish nature. Jun's father, after he returned from America, replaced the geta with the flip-flop of rubber thong sandals. That's what he would wear to go to observe lessons and in the staffroom.

Anyway, I looked on with amusement and interest, for the time being, at the father and son of our household enjoying themselves relaxing together.

I don't know how things will go in the future, but when I look back over the period from Jun's birth until now, it seems certain to me that as Jun has grown up, his father has moved progressively from the position of being simply his father to more that of a friend, placing greater emphasis on their friendship than on their relationship as father and son.

Kawano Yūko from *From the Windows of the Green House*

> puff puff puff
> autumn clouds float by –
> the children
> have gone off to play
> somewhere far away
>
> the eyes
> of the one who has come home
> deep in the night
> and is gazing into my eyes,
> are those of a lonesome man

this person,
who has gone to sleep
clutching
some literature, looks
as weary as a sixty-year-old

muddling together
his wife and children,
the household head grew tired
of scolding us, and
for a while broke off

getting them
to eat proper meals,
having them sleep
on mattresses aired in the sun –
that is my happiness

what is wrong
with being a good wife?
I walk along
stripping berries off
sunlit akamama weeds

Kawano Yūko from Koh

The Tadpole

Jun came home from school with a printed sheet he had been given. On it was written 'Family Life and the Development of the Individual'. When I went to read it, I found it was information about a film on sex education, aimed at fifth graders. For those who wished, there would be a separate day for parents to view this film. I was very keen to see what American sex education was really like. However, unfortunately, that very day we had house guests.

I was looking forward to Jun's return from school the day he was scheduled to see the film. Every day he got home at exactly 3.10 p.m.

This day he stood at the door with his schoolbag dangling from his hand and announced with great seriousness, 'I'm a boy, so soon tadpoles will come from somewhere and fertilise eggs. Anyway, lots and lots of tadpoles will be squirming and swimming around, and dive down inside a sort of thing like a floating balloon below my tummy,' as if he both understood and didn't understand what he was saying.

His tone was so funny that I unthinkingly burst out laughing. It was not surprising. This was the first time since Jun's birth that he had been made aware of such things. As the explanation he'd received was from an English language film, he only partially understood it and hadn't pieced the story together very well. Using the words 'tadpoles' 'fertilisation' 'balloon', he had given his own personal interpretation to the flow of English which he hadn't understood – that was so like Jun.

Thinking he might still have something to say, I stopped laughing. But disregarding me, Jun rushed off outside to play, bat in hand.

Four or five days later, on a Saturday evening, we thought we'd have a barbecue in the garden. In the spirit of campfires, we ate on the grass and chatted in a rambling fashion. At some stage, the topic of our conversation turned to when the children were little. The time they were babies in a nursery. And then we talked about Jun feeling his mother's stomach when Koh was moving around inside it.

That was how it happened that Koh asked, 'How come if I was born from you, Mum, I look like Dad?'

A straight question. Until then, I'd always got away with giving a somewhat vague reply to that question.

The night wind began to get up a little. We set our chairs around the embers and sat in a circle. Everyone was looking into the flames. The flickering colours of the flames made us feel sleepy and nostalgic.

The children's father began speaking in a slow manner. Of the way in which a father's and a mother's bodies are different. Of why children resemble both parents. Of genes and the separation of cells. Of the sac in which a foetus grows. Of how just one of the father's millions of sperms burrows into the mother's egg to produce a child.

'The tadpoles are called semen' and 'The boy thing is called a penis,' interpreted Jun, from his own understanding. The partial knowledge he had just gained from the film he'd seen at school was now making more sense as his father fleshed it out into a concept he could understand, and Jun was so happy.

Koh being Koh, she asked a tricky question. 'Is there a connection between the separation of the cells and things like the birth of Siamese twins and hydatidiform moles?' Koh's knowledge came from the comic she loved to read, *Black Jack*.

Then their father calmly explained the most difficult part, like this: 'When you get married and it's time to make a baby, the father's penis becomes a pump to send semen up into the mother's womb.'

The children seemed somehow to understand, and to accept his caution that because of it they must take good care of their private parts.

They were made to feel, too, that they should ask more if there were things they were still doubtful about, so in turn they put all sorts of question to us. It got so dark we could no longer see each other's faces. We must have sat around the fire like that talking for three hours or more.

Numbers of fireflies flew around flickering their lights among the branches of the trees in our garden. They were blue American fireflies, shining clear and bright, the first fireflies of the year for us.

Kawano Yūko from *From the Windows of the Green House*

> living together
> seventy or eighty
> years to go –
> may my time with you
> pass slowly, slowly

> this tired guy
> who was sleepy, sleepy,
> so sleepy,
> even now, asleep
> he is still tired
>
> a great moon is out,
> floating in the sky –
> in the six-mat room
> is your sleeping form,
> and that suffices for me
>
> Kawano Yūko from Koh

Days When the Children Were Absent

The day after I came home from sending the children off to a camp five hundred kilometres away was my birthday. To celebrate my birthday, we went to see a movie that evening. It was called *Eyewitness*.

The cinema was rather unusual: inside it, at the back, was a café. The seats were sofa-style, around round tables, and a waitress came to take one's order for beer and so on. A cinema with a café attached to it was a novelty for us, and the film was interesting, so we watched it twice through.

It was a real birthday treat, something I hadn't enjoyed for a long while, to sit watching a film just with my husband, from evening until late at night, without worrying about the children.

The house minus the children was totally silent – just like the bottom of a pond. Thanks to the kids' noise being far, far removed, I was able to have my fill of quiet time. Such bliss I experienced for the first time since the children were born. This was my chance, I thought, to spend my days doing whatever I liked. I steadily completed the writing of several manuscripts which were overdue, read crime fiction, and as if this were our second honeymoon, went walking and out to eat with my best pal – how refreshing.

It came to the twelfth day since the children had left for camp. In the intervening days, I had carried out my pleasurable plans one by one. I felt I was enjoying myself while the children were away. But when I thought about it, what I was doing wouldn't really have been different whether the children were here or not. That was because we had settled into a more or less continually carefree rhythm of life anyway.

Which being the case, I wonder what I expected from this period of almost a month of the children's absence. Probably, most of all, some quiet times: in other words, a temporary respite from the endless and time-consuming bustle and clamour of kids.

For, certainly, I was rather fed up of living as the general in charge of everyone's physical and mental well-being, and tired of being stretched to the limit by the children's energy. And yet, this three-sided, noisy way of life, with something new happening every single day – was it not brisk and lively?

Living with children meant that no two days were ever the same: yesterday was completely different to today; today is different from tomorrow; and tomorrow will be different again from yesterday and today. That is the real fun and interest of bringing up children and watching them change day by day.

The tranquillity of life without kids. To tell the truth, I was sick of it after two or three days. No point in just being tired of it; but if only my hands were balanced by those two who were usually with me like weights at dusk, when the sun was just about on the point of sinking and part of the sky was still bright red – ah, that would be good, I thought.

It was rather heart-warming to reflect on my little self using my energy scolding and shouting, while trying with might and main to be a steadfast mast or an anchor for my children. Though it was the kids who were in fact propping me up.

Around the time that Jun was toddling, and Koh was still refusing to be weaned, I left the children with someone and went out for half a day – I felt the same then, too. It was such a strange sensation this sudden freedom and time away from these children who were somewhere around close by me all day long, and from the responsibility I felt for them; my hands seemed pitifully empty.

I had similar feelings while they were away. Yet it was obviously a different situation. When they were little, my whole body and all of my time were entirely devoted to the children. And then, over time, little by little, I got my body and my time back for myself. Obviously that was because the children were growing up and becoming more independent. But this time the children had gone off and left me.

I realised that was how things went. While riding wave after wave of such experiences, parents and children will no doubt be preparing for separation and independence.

Kawano Yūko from From the Windows of the Green House

4

'…how many tens of thousands
more days remain, I wonder'

In Our Frantically Busy Daily Life

'We'll probably die in this house', he says – then, after a pause, 'This is the last house we'll live in.'

Timeline

1986 Nagata published his fourth tanka collection, *The Arrow Cart*.

1990 Kawano became editor of the *Mainichi* newspaper's tanka column.

1991 Kawano published her fifth tanka collection, *Koh*.

1992 Jun entered the English Literature department of Dōshisha University.

1993 Nagata took over the leadership of the Tower tanka society.
Kawano became a selector for the *Tower* journal.

1995 Koh entered the Agricultural Studies department of Kyoto University.
Kawano published her sixth tanka collection, *Time Passes*.

1996 Nagata published his fifth tanka collection, *Fahrenheit*.

1997 Nagata was awarded the Second Terayama Shūji Prize for Tanka for *Fahrenheit*.
Kawano published her seventh tanka collection, *Vital Forces*.

1998 Nagata published his sixth tanka collection, *The Banquet Garden*.
Kawano was awarded the Eighth Kawano Aiko Prize for *Vital Forces*.

1999 Nagata was awarded, for *The Banquet Garden*, the Third Wakayama Bokusui Tanka Prize, and the Fiftieth Yomiuri Literary Prize.
Jun married Yūko Ueda. In August his first son, Kai, was born.

washing the rice
daily cooking it
by your side
how many tens of thousands
more days remain, I wonder

                    Kawano Yūko

this one time
in the world, my family
is together
watching the rain
on the rain eaves

                    Nagata Kazuhiro

palm-of-the-hand size
away in the distance
my husband and kids –
scarlet plum trees and all
I tried scooping them up

at a time when I
was painfully self-conscious,
with no thought
for the length of my stride
you walked at a rapid pace

they are too big,
your strides, I think
as we go along together –
but maybe mine, even now
are too small for you

                  Kawano Yūko from *Time Passes*

in my wife's notebook
when she was young,
the ink has faded
from the address
written over and over

those times when
I walked along, regardless
of the length of your stride,
I was falling
head over heels in love with you

in those days
we walked until we were tired,
walked
until we collapsed,
then went to bed together

Nagata Kazuhiro from *Fahrenheit*

Tears Which Flowed Sideways

Recently, when we were talking on the telephone – I forget the context in which it arose – Baba Akiko said this: 'By the way, at a certain time I gave up being young. I combed my fringe back. I was determined to draw it back tightly. At that time, I'd already made up my mind.'

Baba Akiko was born in 1928, so she must already have been over sixty. How many years had she been wearing her hair drawn back severely, I pondered for a while after I'd put down the phone.

She had sent me the third volume of essays by Nagasawa Mitsu. Dipping into its 'Moon in the Sky', I find a passage which caused me to reread it. 'One day the topic of age was raised in a dialogue with Yoshinaga Sayuri; to the question "When did you accept the feeling that you were no longer young?" she replied, "When my tears no longer flowed straight down my cheeks, but ran sideways," and I was very moved by hearing that.'

'When my tears no longer flowed straight down my cheeks, but ran sideways' – that is the way only an actress would express herself. According to Nagasawa, it was because of 'the way the wrinkles carved into one's face affected the flow of the tears'; for an actress, someone who sells youth and beauty, that was a brave thing to say. When a man ages, he would regard this as wearing a medal. But it's a different situation for a woman. Especially in Japan.

Yoshinaga Sayuri reflected through the cathode ray tube is dazzlingly beautiful, but she too, like Baba Akiko, must someday somewhere have given up on her own youth and been still working.

Everyone thinks they are young. People don't age from inside themselves; it is their external appearance which ages them, isn't it? When people have indications that their figures, faculties, sensitivities are waning, compared to others – that is to say, outwardly, then they are compelled to be 'aged'. There is nothing more ridiculous. However, when you notice, from inside yourself, that youth is departing from your own body, or has already departed, that's the problem.

Baba Akiko said, 'It's more comfortable with my fringe combed back.'

I wonder how women can age gracefully. Perhaps by way of eradicating all excess coquetry, fawning, and gestures, one's persona could appear freshly attractive.

I think it was Kishida Kyōko who spoke of facial wrinkles as a kind of medal; it's interesting that she too is an actress. That is not an expression which turns ageing on its head, but it is a magnificent way of putting it. I myself am over forty. If asked about my age, I'd laugh and answer clearly, without deceit. Something I've noticed recently, is that women who have aged well mostly have bright, clear eyes.

Kawano Yūko from *The Wharf*, issue 18, April 1989

> who were they for,
> those two or three words?
> just now I'm sure
> I heard you giving answers
> in your sleep

this man
he's my spouse
that's why I'm scared!
sometimes he even
becomes invisible

my hands brush
against the clumps
of thick-headed cockscomb plants –
knowing you, knowing only you,
will suffice for one lifetime

it was a day in July
that we met…
you gave me
the tanka journal
with dokudami on its cover

Kawano Yūko from Time Passes

The Tiny Walnut Room

Can't crack an egg. This is a story about my life partner, the boss of our household. We were seeing each other for six years before we married. During all that time, I never noticed. Even after we were married, I wasn't aware for quite a while.

When there isn't any meat or fish to go with the rice, and there's just plenty of hot rice, it's quick and easy and convenient to make a meal of 'rice with raw egg on it' – moreover, that's delicious. Here and there around the table you can hear the sounds of eggs being tapped and cracked open. Everyone's busy cracking eggs, it seems – one can hear the jovial sounds of family members cheerfully setting to and satisfying their hunger.

Amongst them, always last, still holding his egg, is the boss, my husband. He looks uneasy, absurd. He's waiting in silence, with his hand gently outstretched, for someone to do the egg tapping and cracking for him, when they've finished doing their own. Recently, we've all come to understand this. In no time at all, father too will be eating 'rice with egg on', clinking his bowl merrily.

The first time the kids noticed (as I had in the past) this defect of their father's, they were really surprised and made funny faces at each other. Then finally they chanted, 'Heavens, what a baby. Dad is a baby,' delightedly hooting with laughter at him.

Amid the kids' jeering voices and scrutiny, he sat, glowering. He didn't explain why. He looked as if he'd closed his ears and was waiting for the topic of conversation to move on from the egg cracking.

That attitude made us laugh. We almost asked, 'Why on earth can't you crack a simple egg?' but swallowed our words.

Most likely for the man himself, this was no joke. Somehow it was something he couldn't tell people about it; in other words, there was a sort of restraining factor, peculiar to him, in operation which meant he couldn't find the words to explain how he'd come to be unable to crack an egg.

Years and years ago, when we were peeling potatoes together, I'd asked his younger sister why this was so. But she just replied, 'Hmm, I wonder why,' vaguely, and laughed. Probably she herself didn't know the reason.

Though I say he can't crack eggs, hard-boiled eggs are another matter. At times like picnics, he nonchalantly cracks boiled eggs; it's just raw eggs he baulks at. Which being the case, perhaps it's that he has an abhorrence for that slimy sensation you get when you crack open a raw egg. It may be as simple as that.

Yet somehow I find it difficult to ask him straight out; it's now nearly twenty years since we first got together and I still don't know.

'Why can't Dad crack an egg?' asked Koh one time, with a serious face standing in the kitchen doorway.

And I could only reply as vaguely as my sister-in-law had done, 'I wonder why.'

We are a family, so we talk about anything and everything and enjoy being together. We think we know all about each other; it's as if with the touch of a hand we can understand everything. If one of us picks up a hair from the bathroom sink, we recognise it instantly and can say, 'Ha, this is Dad's hair.'

However, because we are a family, there are some parts of ourselves we withhold and leave obscured from our lives together. This issue about eggs is something to which, in the daily life of the household, hardly ever anyone pays attention, it's so insignificant. It's as if that were just a momentary hiccup in the rhythmical flow of everyday life in our home.

In such unexpected crevices, the nooks and crannies of the family's hearts are suddenly visible. It takes a little more than normal concern or sympathy to comprehend the delicate workings of people's hearts.

Late at night I play around, rolling a walnut in my hand. When I get tired of doing that, I insert the point of a knife into a tiny split in the shell and crack it open. Inside the walnut are a number of complex 'rooms'. When I carefully pick out the kernel, I find there is left a kind of brownish skin, dividing room from room. Not unlike the flimsy wings of a large brown cicada. One home, one family. However, each member of our family is separated from the other in the same way as the divisions of a cicada's wings, living as it were in compartments like the walnut's tiny rooms, I sometimes think.

Kawano Yūko from *From the Windows of the Green House*

how poignant
the slackness of his eyelids –
yes, this person
with hair hanging over his forehead
is indeed my husband

your face
as you walk along
with your students –
it's not the face I knew
when we were young

the older he grows
the more he resembles
his father, even to
the way he lingers by me
without saying a word

my last child, Koh
is happy to walk
through crowds,
sandwiched between
her father and brother

it seems like
I've been by your side
for quite a while,
I said, straight-faced
pretending to be a carp

I am peeling
the skin from white peaches…
before long
there will be just the two of us
at such times

saying 'your body
smells of rain',
you bring
your damp-scented body
close to mine

for a little longer
I want to sleep beside you
before I die,
like a firefly,
I'll say

Kawano Yūko from *Vital Forces*

you my husband
turning round to ask me
where the tool box is,
are not really
one of the family

when I see
a finely-sewn seam,
it makes me think
this person's reticence
is a good thing

might you see
behind my ears?
you always approach me
from behind, speaking
over my shoulders

the yellow oxalis
is blooming now
in this world
where I owe you
so much

this man
is shortening his life,
writing –
I hate to see
the grey on his eyelids

if I die first
this man will of course
be in trouble…
not for money, but
for breakfast and dinner

Kawano Yūko from *Home and Family*

passing by the kids
my anger heads straight
for my wife –
the encircled moon
begins to moisten

I grab hold of
that cheeky woman's breast –
the whole thing
witnessed
by my daughter

after I'd raged at my wife
in front of my daughter,
the road
I took to the station
blurred before me

what a sharp tongue
this wife of mine has,
it's exhausting –
I have come to the field
where sunflowers grow

my wife is really
seriously, afraid I'll die
all of a sudden –
should I write of this,
concealing it from her?

she phones me
for no particular reason
when she's depressed –
I should go home soon
this late, rainy night

> now try saying
> 'ra ri ru re ro,'*
> commands my daughter
> at the other end of the phone,
> in imitation of her mother
>
> in the transparent light
> of autumn
> were trembling
> wild chrysanthemums,
> the 'dandoborogiku' flowers**
>
> all you do
> is find fault with me
> for the fatal defect
> of being someone who
> never knew his mother
>
> Nagata Kazuhiro from *Fahrenheit*

Setting up the Tools for Tanka Composition: Time and Place

Composing tanka is not something you can do on days of fine weather, or distracted by noise. Rainy days and cloudy days are good; and with regard to time of day, best of all is the duskiness of twilight, what is called 'the witching hour'.

This witching hour is a time when one's emotions are in a state of flux, one has strangely heightened feelings, and words are readily sparked.

---

* 'Try saying ra ri ru re ro' was a pet phrase of Yūko's. When I'd been drinking, and then phoned home, she would check on me to see if I could pronounce my 'r's clearly. Eventually, our elementary school daughter, Koh, started imitating her. – Nagata Kazuhiro

** I was told about these 'dandoborogiku' by Yūko; they are wild chrysanthemums which grow on Dando Mountain. She liked teaching us the names of wild flowers and grasses which we'd been content to call 'weeds'. – Nagata Kazuhiro

However, twilight is also a time of domestic duties, when one rushes around sweeping the garden and cleaning the bath – oh, there's lots to do – and somehow, with all this brisk movement, poems fly out the window.

It's an excellent thing to sit quite still in this witching hour of dusk, reading and composing tanka; at that time of day, vision is poor and one cannot do anything without an artificial light.

I write tanka at the kitchen table. Ever since I was married, this has been my habit and my way of composing.

Although we have moved house close to twenty times since our wedding, wherever we've lived I've had the feeling that this is just a temporary dwelling place and conducted myself accordingly: I haven't purchased decent crockery for our use; our furniture, too, has been cheap stuff – and I haven't even bought myself a desk. I'm comfortable and happy at the kitchen table, content with that.

With a table and a television installed, it leaves hardly any room to move around, in this small room. There is a great pile of books and letters; flower vases, telephone and the cat are crammed into the kitchen, too. At meal times I put the dishes down amongst all the other stuff. When I'm writing tanka, I add a pencil sharpener and writing materials. Then, when I sit myself down, I am ready to begin work.

Though the room is small, I don't mind using the kitchen table as a desk and it is inconvenient having bookcases scattered all around the place. If I stretch out my hand, I can get the book I need, in this place which is both a kitchen and a study. Dreaming on, I'll probably be using the kitchen table to write my poetry until I die.

Kawano Yūko from the journal *Tanka Research*, June 1995

On my birthday I received a bunch of wild flowers

>getting a messy bundle
>of chamomile and other flowers
>he wrapped them
>in brown paper and
>presented them to me

you, who walk along
parting with your knees
the smartweed ears,
have always been like that,
little brother

twice, while upward circling
on the monkey bars,
you have shown me
the cherry blossoms
at Shōtoku Junior High

        Kawano Yūko from *Home and Family*

many times a day
she laughs, can't stop laughing,
this woman
I am accustomed to
calling 'my wife'

to me and to the cat
she uses different tones of voice –
this evening
she is somewhat gentler
with the cat

as she buries
raw scraps, at twilight
in the paddy
my wife leans
from side to side

what person is this
who acts like my wife
this cold night
writing poetry
with a cloth round her cheeks

names of trees,
names of grasses,
you taught me them all…
a bright winter sun
in the black alder forest

when I don't understand
the reason
for my wife's ill-humour,
I take the kids and the dog
and go out the back door

'eat' she says
then hurries me off to bed –
these days
my ebullient wife
nags me a lot

when she decides
unequivocally
that I'm tired
there's no arguing about it,
and I obey my wife

away from my wild wife
I make something
with our kids –
doing potluck dinner
is a tricky business

on Sundays
when the children are out
you lead
and I follow…
as an owl would

> that you will die
> some day,
> is a thought
> which comes unbidden,
> yellow iris flower
>
> Nagata Kazuhiro from *Fahrenheit*

Moving House

We were going to be moving again. How many times would that make it? This must be the twenty-something time. Even since marrying, I'd moved thirteen times. Our friends and acquaintances have grumbled that it's a chore altering our address in their address books, because it changes so often. Where we are now in Iwakura, is the longest we've lived anywhere. I think this is the eighth year we've been here.

It appears that there are two patterns for people: the settling in one place pattern, and the relocating pattern. I wonder why those people who stay living in a fixed abode don't move. And I wonder what makes those of the relocating pattern come to shift from place to place even when they don't particularly want to. When we were in Yokohama, we lived in an apartment; after six months we changed to the apartment next door. We only lived in America for two years, but even there we moved – that's what I mean.

Each time we've moved, it's been to a different kind of dwelling. Just like its name, the Blue Swamp Court apartment house had a damp miasma. We've also lived in an old-fashioned row of terraced houses. In America, we lived in a house like something out of a picture book: it had green-painted outside walls and a red-brick chimney. At some stage in all this moving around, I became imbued with the sense that wherever we lived was only temporary. So I ended up not buying good quality furniture, having matching crockery, or decorating rooms with nice curtains for the places we lived in. We lived in a sense like rootless weeds of no fixed abode; we'd inevitably move on, one day we'd leave here – that was the feeling I had.

Because of that, I did not want to get closely involved with people in our neighbourhood, or the area itself; thus I preserved a sense of freedom. I'm keenly aware how, for a long time, we have lived fairly carefree and comfortably in all kinds of places.

Our next relocation will be different from the moves till now, which have arisen spontaneously or been a matter of letting things take their course. Because my partner has put his foot down and said, 'I'm fed up now with this way of life.' What he calls 'this way of life' is the way that even when he comes home weary from work, books and scraps of paper are scattered around. The room I'm in is a kind of giant wastepaper basket with notepaper and postcards dangling down like washing on lines strung between the walls. And it is in this room that he is expected to have his meals and relax, watching TV, for instance; in short, he's fed up with this lifestyle. It's because the dining table also serves as my work desk that things are like this.

He has turned fifty this year. He has never minded what I feed him; he's been indifferent as to what I put out for him to wear; all he has done is work. Though he wears two hats – that of a scientific researcher and that of a poet – he has never complained. For such a person to say he's fed up indicates that he had been merely tolerating a great deal until then. For his sake, I wanted to move to a bit bigger house.

Our next house, still in Iwakura, but a little further back, has a large garden and a bamboo grove. While he was cutting useless branches from the old palm tree in the garden, Nagata said, 'We'll probably die in this house,' and then, after a pause, 'This is the last house we'll live in.'

Kawano Yūko from *Kyoto Newspaper*, 3 October 1997

> knowing the whereabouts
> of our registered seal,
> when needs be
> I get it out, that seal
> with your name on

Before our move, the big garden was a wilderness

        saying that we'll die
        in this house, you know,
        he's begun
        chopping useless branches
        off the palm tree

        wondering
        how many grains of rice
        are in one bowl,
        I weep
        as I chew my way through them

        when I must go
        to buy potatoes, I set out
        to buy them,
        this necessity
        a man doesn't understand

        there is never anyone
        in the kitchen, but me
        so
        I eat my meals
        leaning against the rice chest

        I eat some bread
        beside your tiredness –
        as if not to be
        infected by it,
        I'm munching steadily

                Kawano Yūko from *Home and Family*

my wife's voice,
saying the contours
of my face
have slackened,
is a relentless voice

she taught me
the name of those
wild chrysanthemums,
but I simply can't remember
'takasaburō'

looking fragile
with a feverish cold,
my wife stands
in our morning kitchen
dazzlingly lit by the snow

however I slice it
the watermelon only cuts
into triangles –
I wonder how much longer
of this family life

my wife
comes into sight
boredly kicking
some little stones
as she crosses the bridge

fruitlessly
we argued about
sex and love –
from our window
the spread of the night swamp

I am stroking
that throat
without an Adam's apple –
there's a pointlessness
in the feel of my fingers

I'm reconciled
to being gentle –
if I'm kind
about certain things
she will be soothed

my wife
who has had a little hole
pierced in her little ear…
so sad, standing there
in the kitchen

as if to say
on the other side of that door
is the ocean,
you are leaning there now
as you did long ago

you say you are
being sacrificed for the family,
my dissatisfied wife
soaking up to your neck
in bright green spa water

don't telephone me
on rainy days –
rainy day calls
have the lonesomeness
of bonfires

> I tell you
> just that I'm drunk
> and ring off – so
> the receiver that night
> is a heavy lump in my hand
>
> Nagata Kazuhiro from *The Banquet Garden*

At the time I published my tanka collection called *Home and Family*, Nagata asked me – I forget in what context – 'Were you really very lonely?' And I can't forget that.

In our partnership, I chat about anything and everything. When Nagata comes home from work, I'll follow him to the toilet chatting about what's happened, what I've been thinking – all that. Because I talk to him so much, we're a couple who have always, always, stayed close to each other. He, most of all, should understand my loneliness. But then to be asked 'Were you really very lonely?'...

Afterwards, this made me think, all over again, that tanka is a poetic form in which one is going to read feelings which people don't express, can't express, to each other; it's composed on an altogether different level from chatting face to face, personally.

They say the relationships in our family are good. That is true on a certain level; but when we express what lies buried deep in our hearts – it may only be with the slightly differing usage of a particle or an auxiliary verb – then those who write tanka understand each other.

That question from Nagata made me grasp the way the hearts and minds of poets communicate with each other, and the power of the poetic form called tanka.

I'll be happy if even a single reader understands this.

Kawano Yūko from *Silk Tree*, issue 21, June 2002

doubting you will be here
in my final years,
I must relearn
everything about you,
in the manner of déjà vu

                      Kawano Yūko from *To Walk*

with the tap open wide
I create
a solid pillar
from the force of the water,
this night you're not here

the longest we'll have
is thirty more years,
you see…
oh, you respond
from under the elm tree

having been living
with a person who
uses chopsticks nicely,
this evening I noticed
how quiet are his fingers

in your case
the application of the brakes
was good,
I think in all seriousness –
the voice of a morning shrike

selecting tanka
I grow sleepy, but
when I go downstairs
there is a someone else
busy selecting tanka

as you devour
some breakfast bread,
you praise me
for lining up the slices
so cleverly

    Kawano Yūko from *Silk Tree*, issue 21, June 2002

while clumped leaves
of dandelions on the ground
were being drenched,
we became a couple
my wife and I

perhaps she
might be crying?
she's turned away,
been washing those pots
seems like forever

when our son
criticises me, calling me
'distilled water'
my wife sounds like
she's pleased

'you don't reside
in this house,'
she said
unexpectedly,
in a quiet voice

I can't say
I like this recent wife
who wilfully
compares
our son with me

    Nagata Kazuhiro from *The Rough Gods*

I'm often asked
about the strangeness of living
with a scientist,
with someone who cannot eat
his meals properly

I am sitting
waiting on the unlit staircase
today
it is only you who
will come home to this house

when I remark
that these rice cakes
have a Shōwa flavour,
you grunt in reply
as always…

   Kawano Yūko from *Markers of the Seasons*

the bridge sways, and
the swaying quietly spreads –
what you grieve
I too
will be grieving

my wife
shedding her nightdress
like a mythical witch,
is in fine form
this Sunday morning

imagining
the depth of her emotions,
I am in tune
with this person
who quietly weeps

I'll probably say
that thanks to you,
it's been an interesting life…
if it so happens
I die first

    Nagata Kazuhiro from *The Hyakumanben Vicinity*

the bunch of chamomile
flowers I brought home
on Kappaki,*
shrunk and withered,
are hanging in the window

from just two
finally back to two again,
such a short time,
and the long time
thereafter…

as I'm telling her
I wonder if we'll die
in this house,
I set fire
to the pile of fallen leaves

    Nagata Kazuhiro from *The Rough Gods*

---

* Kawano Yūko's birthday was 24 July, the day called Kappaki. Kappaki is the anniversary of Akitagawa Ryūnosuke's death. – Nagata Kazuhiro

5

'in mourning for my breast more than I am'

The Onset of Illness

'I'd been living with him for more than thirty years, and it was the first time I'd seen him look at me with an expression like that'

Timeline

1999   In December, Jun's place of work, Fishing Friend Company, went into voluntary liquidation.

2000   In September, cancer was discovered in Yūko's left breast; in October, she underwent surgery at Kyoto University Hospital, along with radiotherapy. Yūko's eighth tanka collection, *Home and Family*, was published.

2001   Jun set up the Seijisha publishing company; its first publication was Kawano Yūko's ninth tanka collection, *To Walk*.
Nagata published his seventh tanka collection, *The Rough Gods*.

2002   For *To Walk*, Yūko received the Sixth Annual Wakayama Bokusui Tanka Prize, and also the Murasaki Shikibu Literature Prize.
Nagata became the President of the Japanese Society for Cell Biology (a position he held until 2005).
Yūko's father Yukiya died. Yūko published her tenth tanka collection, *My Tanka Diary*. From around this time she was plagued with insomnia and her mental health was also delicate.

2003   Nagata became a selector of the tanka presented for the annual New Year's Poetry Reading at the Imperial Palace. He published his eighth tanka collection, *Wind Direction*.

2004   Yūko published her eleventh tanka collection, *Markers of the Seasons*, and her twelfth, *Garden*.
For *Wind Direction*, Nagata was awarded the Fifty-fourth Minister of Education for Fine Arts, award and also the Thirty-eighth Chōkū Prize.

2005   Nagata became selector for the *Asahi* newspaper Tanka Forum. He published his ninth tanka collection, *The Hyakumanben Vicinity*.

2007   Nagata published his tenth tanka collection, *The Days After*.

2008   Nagata's book *The Life of Protein* was published by Iwanami Shinsho.

> embracing
> the ruin I was
> at that time
> you wept, you could
> do nothing but weep
>
> Kawano Yūko

> 'if I die,
> you'll drown in the bath' –
> that's true
> I will probably
> drown in saké
>
> Nagata Kazuhiro

25 December 1999: Jun's place of work, Fishing Friend Company, voluntary liquidation.

> just there
> in the entrance hall
> our son is standing
> in the cold
> saying nothing
>
> father and son
> wordlessly read through
> and folded
> the salary statement
> I can't bear to read

24 March 2000: cloudy with a cold wind; from morning on Nagata in a bad mood.

>though it's the fall-out
>from his overwork depression,
>what loneliness –
>'don't use my dictionary'
>he growls at me

29 June 2000: cloudy, then rain at Karuizawa; met up with Nagata; we hired a red tandem bike for the morning and rode around.

>this thing does
>go straight ahead then –
>on the red bicycle
>built for two
>vigorously we ride along

8 September 2000: rain for the first time in a while; the rain stopped in the early evening; tonight, too, another night walk with Nagata and our grandson, Kai.

>I want there to remain
>a little more time for me
>to be with you
>in this world, walking,
>pushing the child along

>mine has been
>a happy life I think
>once more,
>yet I am still attached
>to you and mother

20 September 2000: fine; after midnight in front of the mirror I happen to notice

>the great lumps
>in my left armpit –
>what might they be?
>there are two or three
>the size of eggs

> to you facing
> the blue computer screen,
> I say
> 'what are these,'
> and make you touch them

22 September 2000: fine; to the Kyoto University Hospital for the first time in ages; it has been rebuilt, so I got confused; in the number two outpatient clinic for lymph gland surgery, while Professor Shun Inamoto was showing me the ultrasound picture.

> images of three
> jet-black lymph glands
> and of mammary glands –
> 'it's malignant'
> he says, decisively

> right, it was cancer then –
> looking at the ultra-sound
> I think they will
> remove everything, 'cause
> it's spread to the lymph glands

When I was walking along the road beside the hospital, Nagata came from the opposite direction.

> how to describe
> the expression on his face
> looking at me –
> I am here, not
> on a suspension bridge

28 September 2000: fine; to the hospital; Koh came with me; 11 October was decided on for my operation. In the evening, Koh explained things to Nagata for me. I was surprised at her understanding of the disease's rate of development and the operative procedure, and at her ability to recapitulate all that.

> saying 'uh-huh' and 'yeah'
> he nodded, sipping his tea –
> 'build up your strength'
> he said to me
> then went silent

10 October 2000: rain; unable to sleep, I swallow some soporific Halcyon with saké.

> the person who
> is mourning, is in mourning
> for my breast
> more than I am,
> paces about upstairs

11 October 2000: fine; to Kyoto University Hospital; because it was day surgery, what I took fitted in one bag; Nagata accompanied me; the operation was over at 12.04; Nagata came in before one o'clock, but I was still doped from the anaesthetic and didn't open my eyes.

> I hear your voice
> but I am
> a jellyfish
> wobbling in and out
> of sunny shoals

16 October 2000: fine; Koh came home from Kumamoto; felt awful and didn't get up all day; the only work I did was selecting tanka for the *Mainichi* newspaper.

> oh it's so cold
> on my left side
> I want
> a warm body
> to lean against

18 October 2000: fine; two-thirds of my lactation was from the right breast.

> though you pity
> my chest slashed
> straight across
> you say nothing – just
> bathe it in hot water

25 October 2000: rain and cloudy.

> bitterly
> I wept great tears,
> my dishevelment
> witnessed in silence
> by you and Koh alone
>
> 'immerse yourself
> and turn work down!'
> you tell me
> when you've come home
> and are changing the bathwater

Kawano Yūko from My Tanka Diary

> with her swollen gums
> she's baby-faced,
> this wife of mine
> selecting tanka
> chin in hand

> when I am
> thick-headed and sleepy
> my penis swells
> by itself, I told her
> and she laughed

nights when
my wife is absent,
I call our daughter
and ask her nicely
to prepare a meal for me

whatever happens
I absolutely mustn't die
and leave you behind,
she tells me,
holding a dustpan*

first I explain
the difference between
cancer and tumours,
concealing nothing,
not being optimistic

after you have wept
with great sobs,
you are still weeping
and weeping still
you were sharpening the cleavers

it's not something
you can understand,
you tell me
as if throwing down
a trump card jack

as we walk along
I tuck your hand
into my pocket –
how terrible
if you die first

* On 22 September, as the result of an examination at Kyoto University Hospital, Yūko was discovered to have breast cancer. The following Saturday I was working in our garden with her. – Nagata Kazuhiro

from long ago
at your most forlorn times
you have been
so wayward that
I could not help at all

in the plum grove
with its smattering of white
and of crimson blooms,
you say how short
has been our time together

                Nagata Kazuhiro from *Wind Direction*

Suffering From Cancer

Two years ago, on 22 September, I was diagnosed with breast cancer. Two nights previously, I happened to feel in my left armpit and find there three lumps the size of eggs.

I showed them to my husband, Nagata, asking, 'What on earth could this be?'

To which he replied, optimistically, 'You've probably caught some sort of infection.'

I was examined in the Kyoto University Hospital's plastic surgery department, but they sent me straight round to the mammary gland outpatients.

When the doctor in charge saw my mammogram, he said straight out, 'It's malignant.'

I couldn't immediately comprehend my condition. I looked at the jet-black lymph gland images and mammary gland images on the ultrasound plates. Now that I think about it, my personal reaction was quite strange: 'I guess that means something like total removal' was what went through my mind.

When the examinations were over and I was walking along the road beside the hospital, Nagata came from the opposite direction.

I had been living with him for more than thirty years, and it was the first time I'd seen him look at me with an expression like that. His were the eyes of someone seeing something painful. They were the eyes of someone looking at an other-worldly being. Here is the poem I wrote about that occasion:

> how to describe
> the expression on his face
> looking at me –
> I am here, not
> on a suspension bridge

Parting from Nagata, I drove home by the road alongside the Kamogawa river. I couldn't hold back a flood of tears. How much longer had I to live, I wondered. I couldn't help thinking about all the work to be accomplished in my remaining time. The sparkle and glitter of the water's surface in the river, so beautiful. In the vicinity of Demachi-Yanagi, as always there were students walking and going past on bicycles; their youth and liveliness were dazzling to behold. What a bright and lovely place this world is, isn't it, I thought. How was it I hadn't noticed that before? I was so sad. I was more than sad, wanting above all else just to live.

11 October was set as the date for my surgery; I had a lot of work to do, and no time to be swamped by sentiment. Even so, when I bathed alone at night, I wept alone, tears blurring my vision.

> it's an absurd
> and sad thing:
> my nicely shaped
> left breast
> is to be cut off
>
> how many more days
> will you be part of me?
> you were pretty, weren't you,
> I said in the bathwater,
> looking down

The surgery took about three hours and was concluded without incident. They removed about two-thirds of the mammary glands, but left the breast itself. I was so thankful for the skill of the doctors who were able to do that for me. However, the prognosis was poor. The left half of my body felt like it no longer belonged to me. I became terribly susceptible to the cold; my left side was all numb and hard; the area around the wound, and my back, were inflamed with pain. Spring came, and then summer, and still I felt no better. There's a novel by Alexander Dumas, called *The Count of Monte Cristo*, in which the protagonist suffers many years in an iron mask. I seemed to understand the way an iron mask would feel.

The radiation therapy room was in the basement. The first time I went there, I was horrified and thought I must have got the room wrong. In that room were several people with shaved heads; on their heads were purple-coloured lines going in all directions. Then I realised that the purple lines must be there to indicate the exact sites for radiation, as I'd had such lines drawn on my chest.

When I went home later, Nagata looked at my breast criss-crossed with purple lines for radiation, and said, 'Don't show your scars to your mother.' I myself thought I was a pitiful sight.

To sick people, sick people are specially visible. It was very strange that when my illness was at its worst, I caught sight of only very sick people.

One day, in front of the radiation therapy room, there was a transportable bed. Casting a glance at the bed, I saw that it was occupied by a man in his sixties, with a very pale face. The skin was stretched thinly over the bones of his face; he looked so frail, my heart ached for him. All of a sudden, the man opened his eyes; at first he seemed to be looking at me, then his eyes wandered off into the distance. I don't know his name, or who he was. But I have never seen such quiet, transparent eyes. It has been two years since then; most likely he has died. Sometimes I've wondered how this world appears to those who are dying.

A little while after my surgery, I published a collection of tanka.

It was my ninth collection. Usually I anguished a while over the titles of my books, but this time I decided on one immediately: *To Walk*. I didn't consider anything else for the title. For quite a time I couldn't walk in the normal way and had to use a wheelchair. Walking is the most fundament of physical movements – and I couldn't do it. I had a profound sense of the importance to human beings of walking. In exactly the same period when my son's son had passed the milestone of his first birthday and started to walk, I began to walk again, one step at a time. Holding that little child's hand as we walked, I was conscious of the aptness of the expression 'walking practice'. Walking really is a matter of putting one foot after another. I was very happy to receive two awards for *To Walk*: the Sixth Wakayama Bokusui Tanka Prize and the Murasaki Shikibu Literature Prize.

And I am most grateful that in the last couple of weeks the frozen half of my body has finally returned to normal. My body now moves as I wish it to, and I am enjoying my meals again. There can be nothing to surpass this. If my health is good, I can go on to do something in this world. I am slower than most people, but little by little the distance I can walk is lengthening. To walk, to be able to walk. This now, is my joy.

Kawano Yūko from *Western Japan* newspaper,
16 December 2002

>   when I am ill
>   you, who have no idea
>   what proportions
>   of soy sauce and sweet saké to use,
>   broil blue fish for us
>
>   'come on, come on'
>   you tempt me – and I say
>   'I'm coming, I'm coming' –
>   but I wonder if it's far
>   to the Dragon God hot springs

is he really
turning fifty-four soon?
on the back of his hand
as he grips the umbrella shaft
I can see spots

                        Kawano Yūko from *To Walk*

how sad, white cosmos
transparent in sunshine
as I walk with you,
you who are so good
at talking nonsense

on your calendar
there is not even
a little time
which should be
spared for me

all my life
I have loved cats –
I'm more concerned
for the cat than for my spouse,
when I die

what I am afraid of
is you dying –
and I'm sorry for you
being beside me
as I'm dying

                        Kawano Yūko from *Markers of the Seasons*

What I really must do is prolong the life of this person, Nagata Kazuhiro, by even a day. Putting my work aside when Nagata comes home, I'll be waiting with plates warmed and something a bit tasty for him to eat. Poetry takes second place. As long as I feed the kids, it doesn't matter if I leave everything else. Outsiders probably won't believe me but I have hardly looked at the children's academic results. Nothing matters to me more in bringing them up, than that the children are happy. Actually, it would be true to say that I've been placing more importance on Nagata than on the children.

Kawano Yūko from *People I have Met*

> it is not now
> at the end of September
> as the thick darkness
> inches forward,
> that my loneliness has begun
>
> in the brightness
> of a full moon,
> the bush clover by the gate
> parts…there are you
> and Koh, come home
>
> when I die
> I want only my son
> to be with me –
> he won't hold my hand
> he won't cry
>
> forever thinking of me
> as a child-wife,
> he purchases
> the ticket for me
> at Demachiyanagi
>
> if I don't say
> it is rice
> with raw egg on,
> you wouldn't eat
> rice with raw egg on

when I take off
my spectacles, see you
lying there, feet
sticking out from the quilt,
I beat a retreat

husband and son
who act as my guardians
are not here
in the high noon
of the scarlet camellias

this evening, too,
I've finished my dinner alone –
like blind-stitching
is the time
that is left

only you
have stayed by my side –
it's a white peony,
you say,
turning to me

                Kawano Yūko from *Garden*

I berate my wife,
saying 'cut down more'
'decline more work' –
my words to her
are words for me too

in spring
the water level rises
over the barrage –
it's there I've led a person
with a perilous heart

as I adjust my pace
to that of the person
now so easily tired,
we go along up the slope
paved with cherry pistils

irritable
nerves on edge
and lonesome,
my wife has gone to bed
early tonight

so weary,
the whole family
exchanging sharp words…
this cloudy afternoon
swiftly darkens to dusk

   Nagata Kazuhiro from *The Hyakumanben Vicinity*

'more than
he'd miss me, your mother,
your father
would miss you –
don't dare die,' I told my son

now I can say
straight out,
'you are my husband, so
I wanted you to shield me,'
and shut his medical text

you keep on reading
the literature
about cancer cells
without mentioning
my cancer

I chose this man
as my spouse, and
for thirty years
have not made
the tiniest complaint

                Kawano Yūko from *Garden*

the cotton hat
the washed-out hat
of summer –
were you laughing
at that time?

nothing else for it
but to act calm,
yet
that calmness
makes her sad

with sadness I read
your tanka book *Home and Family*,
that home and family
of the time before
you knew about your illness

it's not something to say
while sucking up
buckwheat noodles with grated yam,
but it was fun
meeting you

when I telephone Japan…

      'you've gone to Spain!'
      the surprised voice
      of my wife
      on the other end
      of the telephone line

her existence
has become so fragile –
my wife
descending a Lisbon slope
in the evening sun*

it had always been you
in the passenger seat beside me –
driving
along the Côte d'Or now
in a shimmering heat haze

white plum blossoms
visible here and there,
yet I grieve
at her post-operative
walking pace

suddenly you say
'you have been persevering,
haven't you,'
and my tears drop
onto the bowl of egg rice

whatever happens
first of all learn to forgive!
I say to myself
as I walk along, stripping the ears
from fox-tail grass

I seat her
on the tandem bike
and off we go
past the train station
to the Gentian Library

* In 2001, after her surgery, my wife accompanied me to the European Molecular Biology Conference. Then we toured from Lisbon in Portugal to Bourgogne in France. – Nagata Kazuhiro

a red bicycle
built for two, and
morning coffee
that summer
at the Manpei Hotel

for your birthday
I chose some wild flowers,
buy them
and go home to you
so prone to depression lately

I have tried
not to lament
at the same level
as you – does that
give you grief, too

I must not say
my concern is deeper
than yours,
now that we have
got through these two years

I've spent the days
wishing to make
the most sense
of my life – and you
condemn those days?

stubbornly
continuing to refuse
any sympathy,
I have barely
held myself together

one small word
of kindness would
most likely sink me
instantly – that's
what I feared

        Nagata Kazuhiro from *The Days After*

over there,
ah, and over there,
you exclaim
pointing at the remainder
of the mountain cherry blossoms

were you lonely
that's why you went to bed first?
our daughter
indicates to me
the clumsiness of my response

suddenly weeping,
weeping so your face seems
to turn inside out…
I'm confused, recoil
from this person

this night you
are over-excited, having fun
I am left behind
in my loneliness,
feeling ill-tempered

from you, on that slope
climbing up the rainy mountain,
I first learned about
the wild chrysanthemums
called 'dandoborogiku'

you are the only mother
of these two children
who have come rushing
with concern for you,
over the last few days*

'continuing to wait,
growing tired of waiting,
I am so sick' –
those sorrowful words
come straight at me

I will be with you
till the end, I'll never leave you,
go quickly to sleep…
now, while the medicine
is taking effect

> Nagata Kazuhiro from *Fair Weather*

finally
a day of sanity, today
having walked the tightrope
I'll go to bed early
and escape from everyone

I lost consciousness
under the poisonous drug,
with my family
there beside me
pouring hot water

---

* From around 2002, several times a year, Yūko was beset by serious bouts of mental instability. She suffered both from insomnia and excitability. Every night, endlessly repeated outbursts of rage and fighting words, which had me numerous times sending out an SOS to our children, to summon them.– Nagata Kazuhiro

the day that
I ended up hurting
this person so much,
all of my tablets
were white, but...

                      Kawano Yūko from *The Garden*

alongside me
the man's body is warm,
much warmer
than it appears,
this paulownia tree

how shall I start telling you,
takasaburō flower,
that the moon
will not come out
for a little longer

coming back
to our home where
camellias are in bloom,
you show pity
for my swollen cheeks

let's ride on
all the way to the terminus,
you say –
oh, that's fine
no one else is here

I don't understand –
however
you are the scholar,
writing something there
so vigorously

it was by mere chance
that we encountered
one another –
so very yellow,
the evening primroses

sinking beneath
a mountain of postcard
tanka submissions,
Nagata Kazuhiro
the yawning god

will he be so weary
he'll sleep
until the day he dies?
I really pity
Nagata Kazuhiro

how insensitive I was!
now, slowly
and steadily
I'll keep writing down
what you say

                        Kawano Yūko from *The Reed Boat*

The Sleepy Person

It was not long after we began seeing each other. On the platform of the Keihan Shichijō station, Nagata saw ornamental cabbages growing. 'Ah', he said pointing at them, 'cabbages', which surprised me a lot. He was pretty much a botanical ignoramus, but since meeting me, a lover of plants, he has come to understand a little about them.

But, no mistake about it, he is still quite ignorant. Recently he told his students, as if he were an expert interested in such things, 'This is a spring wild flower called nogeshi. The difference between that and autumn nogeshi is that the spring variety blooms with its head drooping.' However, what he was talking about was the difference between two other flowers, varieties of asters.

Each year, when spring comes, I explain to him, 'Look, this is a spring aster. Its head droops a bit and it's pale purple in colour.' No matter how many years I repeat this information, he forgets.

It's the same case with the wild chrysanthemums called dandoborogiku. That is a plant discovered on Dando mountain in Aichi Prefecture, and it's an immigrant to the area. Around there the dandoborogiku grow readily, almost like a kind of weed. This year, too, they are rustling in our garden and the grove, but he never notices them. About the time he had just learned the name, dandoborogiku, Nagata composed this tanka:

> in the transparent light
> of autumn
> were trembling
> wild chrysantehmums
> the 'dandoborogiku' flowers
>
> Nagata Kazuhiro from *Fahrenheit*

Apparently the name appealed to him and he chanted it in his tanka like a spell – yet he didn't recognise the real thing when he saw it.

This sort of thing is not limited to plants. We have been married over thirty years; I'm stumped that he doesn't know Pacific saury from sardines.

When autumn comes and I put before him a plate of broiled fish, I explain, 'This fish has a narrow, pointed, head, see. It's called Pacific saury.'

'Yes,' he agrees and eats it without question.

As far as clothing goes, too, when I say, 'Please wear this today,' without a second thought he agrees and puts it on to go out.

When I say Ruru tablets for your cold, take three, put them on his palm and pass him a glass of water, he thanks me and swallows them down with a drink. In all such respects, this man, Nagata Kazuhiro, more obedient than a child, is really lovable.

Not remembering a woman's face, may, in a certain sense, be fatal. A constant happening is that he'll introduce himself and say 'How do you do' when greeting someone he has already met any number of times; then the other party might respond to the effect that this in fact is the third time of meeting. This happens over and over. I'm embarrassed at the large number of people he has annoyed and hurt this way. The man himself is conscious of his fault, but the fact is that he doesn't register faces, and it's probably too late to do anything about this.

Quite a long while after we were married, he gazed at my face and amazed me by saying, 'Heavens, you've got dimples.' We'd been together for five years – where had he been fixing his gaze? And yet, it is fascinating that when looking at old photographs, he can pinpoint exactly who is in them.

The structure of Nagata Kazuhiro's face is not something which I consider on a daily basis. Some years ago, I accompanied him to an academic meeting in Budapest. I was surprised when he let fly with jokes during the introduction to his speech, and had the audience in frequent bursts of laughter. When I watched him up there on the stage, I saw that face of his, which in Japan has a demon-like, uncomfortably hot appearance, as something magnificent amongst the foreigners. Hah, it's his hair and eyebrows that do it. The man himself is rather self-conscious about his hair and eyebrows; but since that time in Budapest I say to him, 'You're fine – if you took away your hair and eyebrows, all that would be left would be your eyes.'

I wonder how long it's been since white hairs began to be noticeable mixed among the dark hairs in his outstandingly thick eyebrows. Although he's a year younger than I, his white hairs have been multiplying for a number of years now. In his youth, Nagata had bushy jet-black hair which stood straight up; but recently some curly grey hairs are having their own way on his head.

When I stand in the entry, seeing him off to work, I'll say, 'Comb, darling, comb.'

Then he'll run both hands over his head and get his hair messier. It doesn't matter whether he combs it or not, his hairstyle hardly changes. Should I delight in this, or sorrow over it?

> with his hair
> like dried out
> leek roots,
> Nagata Kazuhiro
> came sauntering along

Hanayama Shūko from *Tower* journal, November 2003

This was the tanka which was made about Nagata at the Tower society's national meeting three years ago. It's so amusing, I laughed; but when I thought of what is most likely to happen in the near future, I shuddered. It can truly be described as 'hair like dried-out leek roots'. He used to have some soft curls, but, yes, these days his hair is more like sapless, wrinkling leek roots. Hanayama Shūko is a painter, so she probably has a different, painterly point of view.

I first met Nagata Kazuhiro when he was still only nineteen years old. He accepted me as I was – fragile and somewhat unstable in mind and body – telling me I was fine by him, like that. Those words set the pattern for Nagata's and my lives, one could say.

We've been living together a long time now; as husband, father of my children, son of my parents, Nagata is peerless. My son has three children, aged seven, four, and seven months, respectively. Whenever we go to visit their home, they fly straight to Nagata with cries of joy; I am only his appendage. My role is to stand to one side beaming smiles at them – and that's okay by me, I guess. Children have a certain sense of smell which makes them chose mellow human beings, so it can't be helped.

When our children were little and we had time and strength, we used to often go for picnic lunches in the mountains around Kyoto. We even went as far as Shinshū to gather mushrooms. We always took rice balls with pickled plums in the centre; and always, after we had finished eating the rice balls, Nagata would say exactly the same thing as he chucked away his plum stone.

In all seriousness, he'd tell the stone, 'Grow into a plum forest here and we might come to see your blossoms when you flower.'

Then I would say, 'Darling, nothing will sprout from a pickled plum,' but he still believed it could happen.

I really wondered at this thinking on the part of a scientist, but he went on calmly believing for years and years that something could grow from a pickled plum.

One year or other by some chance he said, 'Hey, how about digging to make a spa in the garden? What a great luxury it would be to have a hot spring bath at home every day,' he instantly added.

It seems he passed on the idea of such nonsensical concepts to Koh, because she, in turn, said to me seriously, 'Mother, let's keep goats in the garden.'

Nagata Kazuhiro was twenty-nine when he resigned from the Morinaga Milk Industry's Central Research Institute and came back to Kyoto University. His thinking apparently was that, once he was thirty, he wouldn't be able to move, so he should do it while he was still in his twenties. Jun was three, and Koh was one. Although I say 'returned to the university', it was only as an unsalaried researcher. There were no guarantees for the future. Looking back on it now, it was a reckless thing to do, but at the time it seemed no big deal – I wonder why.

We moved and went to live in a row of three houses near the Ninnaji temple in Kyoto. In order to make a living for the household, Nagata became a teacher at a cram school. By the time he'd taught at the cram school and done his work at the university, it was usually midnight before he got home. He'd eat his meal. Then, with the mill between his thighs, grind some coffee beans, all the time tweaking tanka little by little. Then we would drink coffee facing each other, with our legs under the kotatsu heater and together work on composing tanka and writing articles until morning came. We quarrelled repeatedly. Sometimes in the end I'd pack up the kids and go home to my parents' house.

More than thirty years have passed since that time; however, there has been no change in our lifestyle pattern of starting work on tanka late at night. Nowadays we have become much much busier. Living alongside someone who doesn't take O Bon or New Year holidays, or have weekends at leisure, is extremely stressful and my nerves get very strained.

There's a simple, common saying 'two pairs of straw sandals'.* Applying himself earnestly for decades to the two very different fields of science and tanka, and giving them equal consideration, has been a great labour for Nagata. All these years I have hardly ever heard him complain, or wail about this. However, as he breathes beside me I keep hearing him mutter, 'I'm sleepy, so sleepy.' Virtually all I can do for Nagata who lives like this, is to keep him well-fed. If I were to say to him, 'Your life could be summarised by that one word, "sleepy", and "sleepy" will be your only legacy,' maybe he'd get angry with me.

Nagata couldn't care less about food, but he's a bit of a stickler about saké. In his youth he'd drink a 1.8-litre bottle of saké at a time. Anyway, he drank a lot. Takekawa Chūichi used to say Nagata worked too much and drank too much; that's certainly true. In addition to saké, Nagata loves wine. We must have several hundred bottles of wine in storage. He has purchased any number of books about wine. He organises his wine cellar by writing, without fail, the name of every bottle of wine he opens, in a notebook which he keeps by the bedside. When he pours high-quality wine into a glass, the look on his face says that there can be no greater bliss in life than this. It's a shame that I, Nagata's partner, don't really appreciate wine. When he swirls some wine in a glass and makes comments like 'This is an Italian wine, it has a mossy fragrance' or 'This one has the aroma of wet leaves' or 'Oh, the taste and scent have gradually unfolded,' then hears me give a drunken grunt in response, it must seem as if his bliss is contagious. The dishes we eat to accompany the wine are more or less set: either steak with tartare sauce, fried cod or seafood salad. And sometimes we'll have smoked salmon or creamed broccoli soup as well. I'm grateful that he is satisfied with this sort of menu, which is relatively quick and easy to prepare.

* Translator's note: equivalent to the English saying 'wearing two hats'.

Since I had surgery for breast cancer six years ago, Nagata's feelings toward me have changed significantly. For the first time since we were married, he is seriously concerned about the fact that he does not know when I will no longer be by his side; and it seems to me he has probably come to the point where he is giving deep consideration to the situation. And I am, too.

'Don't tire yourself, cut down on your work, go to bed early,' he has got into the habit of saying to me.

> easily
> forgetting about things
> and going on living
> is not negligent –
> a turtle at high noon
>
> never knowing
> my mother, motherless
> these fifty years –
> snow falls on the lake
> and falling, disappears
>
> Nagata Kazuhiro from *The Hyakumanben Vicinity*

Since I became ill, the number of tanka he writes about turtles, and about his birth mother, whom he lost at the age of three, has increased.

Kawano Yūko from *Tanka* journal, October 2006

> that man who understands
> when I say moonlight
> is perfumed –
> where has he gone off to
> carrying his briefcase

I've a husband
who is like an older brother
and like a father, to me –
from time to time
he strokes my head

I'm pleased to be told
I have cute dimples,
and my husband
is innocently more pleased
for me, than I am

make a speech,
you tell me, so here I am
at the meeting
of the Social Education Committee
of Kyoto city

no good with a corkscrew...
'hey you, someone,'
I call out
to the only other person
in my household

this man of mine
is becoming
more and more childlike,
clad only in underpants
he's eating watermelon

these last five years
I have spent beside you
trying
to prolong my life
one day at a time

I have been
a good wife to him, I think –
in the breeze
from the fan set on 'low',
my hair flutters

I am so glad
to have been born
a woman –
for the children and you
I'm warming some milk

I want the body I had
before my illness,
the body of a woman
with the scent
of earth after rain

that young you
who used to act so cool
strolling along
umbrella unfurled,
I'm chasing you

        Kawano Yūko from *The Maternal Line*

when I call your attention
to a chinch bug on the stone wall
where, here and there
tea-flowers are in bloom,
you turn around

I've brought with me,
to this northern hot spring,
the person
who wanted to seclude herself
during her post-illness phase

if you say
you would like to laugh,
shall I continue
telling my silly jokes
as far as that corner

sullenness is
immediately evident
in my expression –
that's so immature,
says my wife critically

I don't know
the reason why
but
I'm so, so worried,
she calls me to say

if you would only
let it go, life could be
quite pleasant –
worrying and worrying
you will be ill again

Nagata Kazuhiro from Good Weather

that time afterwards,
the time when I lived in fear
of cancer recurring,
passed before I realised
the silk tree was in bloom

if I'd had
an elder brother,
he would have hated
Nagata Kazuhiro –
I'm sure of that

I cook the rice –
until the day I die
I want to be me,
able to cook the rice
for whomever

                Kawano Yūko from *The Reed Boat*

6

'I will die as your wife'

Cancer Reappears

'…I wonder how many injections I have had over the past ten years into those veins, and feel sorry for my right arm. The right side of my body has been shielding the left side. My family also has been my "right" side. And will always be, for as long as it takes.'

Timeline

2008 Kawano Yūko became a selector of the tanka presented for the annual New Year's Poetry Reading at the Imperial Palace.

For his collection *The Days After*, Nagata was awarded the Nineteenth Saitō Mokichi Prize For Tanka.

In July, Yūko's cancer recurred; it was discovered to have metastasised.

In September, Yūko's mother, Kimie, died.

In November, Yūko's thirteenth tanka collection, *The Maternal Line*, was published.

2009 For *The Maternal Line*, Kawano Yūko was awarded the Twentieth Saitō Mokichi Prize for Tanka, and the Forty-Third Chōkū prize.

Nagata published his eleventh tanka collection, *Good Weather*.

Yūko published her fourteenth tanka collection, *The Reed Boat*.

2010 For *Good Weather*, Nagata was awarded the Tenth Yamamoto Kenkichi Prize for Literature.

In April, Koh was married.

The family cat, Tom, left the house and never returned.

every day
I laugh, again and again,
so that I can leave you
my laughing voice
and my laughing face

         Kawano Yūko

each day passing
subtracts one day
from the time
I will have with you –
soon the summer solstice

         Nagata Kazuhiro

16 July 2008, at Kyoto University Hospital

unmistakable:
three sites of metastasis –
has the cancer
finally come back, I ask
my treating physician

just as I am
sobbing my heart out,
you come home
and in silence
stroke my back

though you are anxious,
much more anxious
than I,
the suffering body
is my body

saying 'don't you dare
die before me',
wearily
you fall asleep
still wearing your socks

it is I alone
who have embraced you,
a sadness
which has protected me,
over these forty years

how much more time
is remaining for me
to be with you
in this home of ours,
answer me, beams!

in about as long as
it takes to wait
for the next train,
I came across you
in the time of this world

Kawano Yūko from The Reed Boat

we do know
you've been weeping,
say inokozuchi weeds
which follow me
and are spilt on the floor

though I understand
the words you want
me to say,
if I say them
you will likely drown

that afternoon
in the chair
silently weeping –
was it you
or was it I?

we never doubted
that for you
and for me
equal time
would remain

people say time
has passed in a flash –
shorter than that
will be our time
from now on

you won't forget
and I won't forget
that for your birthday
I gave you
chamomile flowers

shall I make
some chamomile tea, I say –
so frail, our garden
under a hazy sun
this afternoon

in the twilight
the mistletoe
casts deep shadows –
I was too happy,
she says, weeping

summer rain
falls into the precious time
of this world
where you are here
and I am still here

I do hate being alone
like a single circle
of water
floating in a pool,
let me tell you

in the afternoon
as she is sleeping
hooked up
to an intravenous drip,
a soft rain falls

these cherry blossoms
cherry blossoms that day,
all of them, all of them
I have seen with you
the cherry blossoms of Kyoto

Nagata Kazuhiro from *The Summer 2010*

My Illness

I was diagnosed with breast cancer in the autumn of the year 2000. Since that time, I have not had a single tranquil day. At the onset, I thought optimistically and simplistically, 'If I have surgery it should be okay,' which was absurd. I came to realise that surgery for breast cancer was only the start of my real illness.

For the last ten years, I have suffered continuously, worrying if the cancer might metastasise or recur, and beset by unexpected after-effects of the surgery. As the surgery was on my left breast, it was on my left side that I have had the after-effects. From the top of my head to the tips of my toes, I've been numb and cold. Even in the middle of summer, I felt ridiculously chilled. My chest and back were frozen like a solid block of rock. Although they were both parts of my same body, it was as if even the right side of my body couldn't comprehend the pain of my left side. So it was from the start impossible for other people to understand this. One cannot comprehend mental or physical suffering, even one's own; that is the nature of human beings, I came to realise.

I tried everything I could think of: swimming, balancing, massage, acupuncture, yoga, pain clinics – nothing helped. I would be afflicted with these after-effects until I died.

Eight years after the surgery, in the summer of the year before last, I was informed by my doctor that I had three sites of metastasis. Hearing this I was quite calm. I did not take in the real awfulness of my illness until I had begun chemotherapy. Cancer, they say is a fight against its side effects. Truly that is so.

The same year in spring, my mother had developed cancer in her ovaries and pancreas; she was in the final stages, and I was informed it was too late for anything to be done about her cancers. For a while after her hospitalisation, mother was cared for at home; as often as I could, I went to visit her there, in Shiga, where I had lived with my parents and sister. It was very hard watching my mother growing weaker each time I saw her. She literally withered away.

Mother was often vague and she had dementia; but when it was just the two of us, I cupped her cheeks with my hands and put my forehead against hers. I wept and she asked me in a little voice, 'Is something the matter in Kyoto?' It saddened me to realise that she was forgetting her own woes, so great was her concern, as a mother, for her daughter's troubles.

Her hands and face were cold, and her body so thin it was difficult to conceive of it as being human. Death was certainly approaching and there was nothing anyone could do to halt it. In her days of health, mother had told me that dying was a major task; now she had begun that final major task. All alone.

I myself had lost all the hair from my body as a result of the side effects of the anti-cancer drugs I was given; the extremities of my hands and feet had become numb and I couldn't feel with them; I often dropped things. I was so washed out that I was either vague or confined to bed; when I was home alone I would sort of cave in and be incapable of thought.

My hair finally grew back, soft, baby-like hair, which I patted affectionately. However, when the medication was changed, my hair fell out again. What really undid me was the inability to eat.

When I became unable to perform the natural act of eating, I began pondering on things I had never really considered before, like animals being killed and plants being robbed of their lives, just so that people could eat, so that they could live. (Probably I had previously deliberately wiped such issues from my mind.)

I couldn't manage anything firm. I had to depend for my nourishment entirely on soup, an unbalanced diet. While I was bedridden for eight days, I became unable to walk. Knowing that wouldn't do, I ended up setting myself to practise walking – how pitiful. Things that I thought of as only happening to others were happening, in succession, to me; and I felt keenly the words of people from long ago.

How fragile and short is human life. But it couldn't be true. In my parents' lineage, people were long-lived.

So, recklessly and arbitrarily I imagined that I, too, would have a long life. Masaoka Shiki, in his book *My Six-foot Sickbed* wrote that having an invalid in the house is the same as having a war break out there – and it really is like that. On account of my illness, the members of my family grew weary in body and soul. With their nerves hypersensitive, they often argued over nothing all. And yet because they were family, they protected me and listened to whatever I had to say. When there is something major going on in a home, both the hitherto good and the bad aspects of the family finally appear.

The most immediate worry was obviously that I could not eat. Things like going to the movies or the theatre, or travelling, have always involved the pleasure of eating delicious foods at various places.

There isn't a single day I don't wonder how many more years I am able to live. When I take a bath, I'll look at the veins in my right arm and wonder how many injections I have had over the past ten years into those veins, and feel sorry for my right arm. The right side of my body has been shielding the left side. My family also has been my 'right side'. And will always be, for as long as it takes.

In some TV dramas, the story goes that it's a good thing to have developed this illness and they apparently end that way. But I would not put it so simplistically. Becoming ill has never done me any good. However, coming in contact with people who are sick in mind and body, I have become able to feel true empathy with them.

I am happy that the season is moving towards brighter days. The nights when I am so anxious that I can't sleep, continue; but at such times I set myself to recalling all the blossoms I have seen in my life. And then I try enumerating what flowers seeds we might sow in our garden. Cosmos and morning glory, of course. This year I definitely want to plant some Imperial dahlias. I haven't actually seem them myself, but I've heard that they can grow up to the second storey of a house, and will produce pale purple blossoms until the frosts come. Imperial dahlias, their name alone is enchanting.

Thinking happy thoughts as much as I can, I will walk towards the radiance of the sun.

> I'll sow the seeds
> of lots of morning glories,
> cosmos too –
> fair seasons will come
> and they will flourish

Kawano Yūko from *Clear Stream* journal, June 2010

> I will go on living,
> live my life right through
> to the end –
> after that, it will be
> up to you what you do

staying by me
as I'm getting ugly,
you would say
'it's a good thing
I've had you'

rather than die as a poet,
I shall die
as the mother
of these children,
and as your wife

'not even five years' –
your words this morning,
probably true
though my doctor
doesn't say them

definitely good that
it's taking me years and years
to die, while I
just make your meals
and compose tanka

'don't die,' you say
in the same rough way
you'd use
talking to a male friend –
white touch-me-not flowers

for me, there will be
no days in my seventies –
I feel sad
for you living
those days I shall not

Kawano Yūko from *The Reed Boat*

only your voice
always sounds healthy,
only I know
what has gone on
before you end the call

the times when
you tell me you're frustrated,
that frustration
becomes mine, too –
November rain

to your whispered
'five more years, if only…'
I murmur agreement,
in my heart denying
that possibility

I promise
I won't undertake any more
manuscripts –
my time with you now
is such a little time

unable to take
upon myself, your sickness,
I go out to the garden
and just call to you
'snow, it's snowing'

Yūko had written this:

> no one to say
> 'I'll take that sick body
> for you' –
> dandelions
> puff, puff

although of course
I know full well
the side effects,
there's no way we will say
'let's stop the treatment now'

the days for us
to spend together
are numbered, it's true,
and in my final years
you will not be here

though I don't know
whether or not we were
a good couple,
we probably were
an interesting couple

'don't trample the cosmos,' again
her voice flies through the air –
that voice
I hear at my back
is the voice of long ago

her tanka will stay
and probably I'll cry
over those tanka,
when the day comes, sometime
that sometime I fear so much

Nagata Kazuhiro from *The Summer 2010*

the white bush-clover
has already begun to bloom
trailing along the gate …
waiting for you, means
being awaited by you

this man
is an untidy sleeper
like a child –
I roll him over
and pull his coverlet up

there is no guarantee
that you will be there
when I die –
you are out in the garden
burning fallen leaves

the day I saw
white cosmos in Michinoku,
I was healthy
and you were there
by my side

heading for Wakasa,
you have left –
were I well,
I'd have gone with you
across the Hanase Pass

patting my head
two or three times
you set off
amid the heat
that followed the 'Great Heat'

          Kawano Yūko from *The Voices of Cicadas*

The Rice Bran Bed

Even after I had come home from hospital, there was another month of days when all I could eventually get down was half a cup of milk a day. My weight had dropped to thirty-three kilos. The Princesses and Prince Kashiwagi in *The Tale of Genji*, we read, were unable to eat fruit, so they grew weak and died. Without an intravenous drip, I would certainly have died sooner or later. The drip delivered 950cc over half a day, and I had subcutaneous injections in my stomach on an ongoing basis to prevent me vomiting. That drip was literally 'the water of life'.

As I lay in bed unable to eat, naturally what I thought about was food.

When I was a senior high school student, there was a great fig tree growing over the roof of my family home. Every autumn we would boil three or four big pan-fulls of figs and make fig jam. In my family, we called the broken-off tips of bamboo 'praying hands'. We'd use one of these to get the fruit from the tree. How delicious they were, those well-ripened, freshly picked figs.

The taste of that eggplant pickled in rice bran which we ate at home after morning exercises done to the radio, when I was in fifth and sixth grades of elementary school. That was for sure the most delicious taste. With a tender yet crisp texture and imbued literally with the colour of eggplant purple, these eggplant pickles had a slightly sour tang. We would add grated ginger and eat them dipped in soy sauce. Blended with the fragrant smell of rice mixed with wheat, they're an unrivalled combination.

Ever since then, I have been making eggplant pickles year after year and I'm still enjoying them. In fact, they're so delicious I've often ended up eating too much rice (so that I could have more pickles). So one summer I ventured not to make the pickles. Now I've given over the rice bran bed to my husband and daughter, but I annoy them by continuing to tell them, 'Mix it up, mix it up, won't you.' The things in our rice bran 'bed' are rice bran, salt, red pepper, leftover beer, smoked and dried bonito, kelp and the shells of about three eggs. This year's produce is not far from the best.

In the pickling shed at my parents' home, there were any number of pickling tubs containing white cabbage and daikon radishes and so on. Alongside them was the rice bran pickling pot. Kept cool, my mother's rice bran bed was smoother than mine, with a nice scent. To the touch and smell of someone experienced, my rice bran bed doesn't match up to hers.

Taking good care of, giving love, and stroking. Taking time. These things will bring rewards to the wife, mother, and keeper of the home. I am hoping and praying that my rice bran bed will stay safe and in good condition through the coming years.

Kawano Yūko from the *Sankei* newspaper, 24 July 2010

> you will live through
> days of sadness
> unknown to me –
> though I feel for you,
> to console you is so hard

> the voices
> of my husband and daughter
> reach me in bed –
> I can't die and leave
> such a lovely family

Kawano Yūko from *The Voices of Cicadas*

> my husband and children
> approached my pillow,
> their voices as faint
> as firefly lights –
> I must not die

> oh why
> do you weep like that
> when you look at my face?
> I won't die –
> but Tom did die

my body is no longer
a body which can
go anywhere –
the words of this body
leaving you behind

Spoken by Yūko and transcribed 8–9 August 2010

House Calls

I don't know myself how much longer I can live. People say 'until the time the cosmos bloom', 'perhaps you'll get through to next year', 'until this time next year', and so on; but it's not something I can know. My mother was told 'another month', then she lived for six months longer; when I reflect on that, I think it's best to look on the optimistic side.

The easy, everyday things I used to be able to do, like walking and writing, have become impossible for me, which is all the more of a burden for my family now; if I could just get a little better, we'd be able to get by.

I'm relying on my husband and son and daughter to write things down for me, and their pens move more smoothly than I would have thought. This manuscript is being transcribed by my husband.

When it was decided that I would be cared for at home, I thought it would not be a simple matter. At shower times, I could have no hesitation in showing this poor body of mine. Or when having suppositories inserted, either.

Each time I was washed, or wiped, or helped to drink tea, the words 'thank you' automatically came to my lips. Come to think of it, since I've been back at home the number of things I'm having done for me has multiplied, and I've noticed that they are all done through the medium of people's hands.

When I read Masaoka Shiki's sickbed diary, I had noticed that such expressions as 'had something or other done for me' were extremely numerous. But I could never have imagined that one day I would be having the same expressions transcribed for me.

The current situation is this: every two or three days the doctor in charge of my treatment comes to do a house call, carrying a big bag. Nurses are rostered to come in each day. So I am receiving perfect, personal nursing care.

It's wonderful that my doctor does these house calls for me. Probably a few decades since I've experienced medical examinations at home, yet they have a sense of familiarity. Once upon a time, I recall, the doctor used to bring a nurse with him on house calls. At the patient's house the family prepared a basin of hot water, and so on. That kind of interaction between urban doctors and their patients produced a warm, close relationship, and will probably still do so. This is my own experience right now. When I was hospitalised, I felt like I was on a conveyor belt, but now it is all one-on-one care. There is warmth in both the way the doctor asks his questions, and the way he examines me with his stethoscope.

Kawano Yūko from Sankei newspaper, 7 August 2010
(extracted from Family Poems)

> kneeling beside me,
> you beg me not to die –
> your bent neck
> as you weep
> is that of a child

> today my husband
> three times in tears said
> 'please don't die,'
> and three times in tears saying
> 'please don't die,' went off to his school

Kawano Yūko from The Voices of Cicadas,
spoken by Yūko and transcribed 8–9 August.

though I feel
I want you to live on
for my sake,
it is you who will be
the most bereft of all

enumerating
this one and that, for whom
I wish a long life,
finally I add you
solitary you, to the list

                Spoken and transcribed on 10 August

7

Last Writings and the Time That Was Left

At seven minutes past eight in the evening, on 12 August 2010, Kawano Yūko died from breast cancer.

> though I understand
> so well, the feelings
> of each of you,
> how few words there are
> to leave you with, now
>
> in this lonely
> yet warm world,
> it was my good fortune
> to be able to meet you,
> so I believe
>
> shall I die in August?
> cicadas' songs
> pouring down
> with no discrimination
> between morning and evening
>
> reaching out my hand
> I want to touch you all,
> my dear ones – but
> I haven't enough breath,
> not in this world

> Kawano Yūko from *The Voices of Cicadas*,
> spoken by Yūko on 11 August and transcribed

The Time That Was Left – Nagata Kazuhiro

22 September 2000. I can never forget this date. If there is such a thing as a plan for one's life, then the plan can go completely wrong – the first sign of that for me raised its head on 22 September 2000.

Basically, I don't keep a diary. Any number of times I have tried to take up the challenge of keeping one; somehow my efforts never continue for long; the longest would have been about six months, before all too soon I downed tools. It's not simply a matter of being lazy: for us poets, rather than an ordinary written diary, it is the record we keep in our hearts which is far more vivid; the important thing is that we have, in the form of tanka poetry, a means of recording our deepest emotions.

And yet, most unusually for me, I still have the diary for the month which followed that fatal date. Perhaps because the shock was so great, and I realised it was a truly serious matter for me, I felt I should leave a record of this in diary form.

Here is what I wrote in my diary that day:

22 September

Went out in the car with Yūko and Koh, to take Yūko for an examination at Plastic Surgery Outpatients. Two days previously (on 20th), Yūko herself had noticed big lumps, each about the size of a ping-pong ball in her armpit, and had showed them to me. Touching them, I could feel clearly defined round lumps there. Yesterday when I talked at my laboratory with Ms N (a postgraduate student who has come from the Plastic Surgery Department to do PhD research), she telephoned Professor Yoshihiko Nishimura at Plastic Surgery for me, and arranged a special examination for Yūko with him for today.

After midday, there was a phone call from Professor Nishimura: he says that the lumps in Yūko's armpit are swollen lymph glands. There is a fairly strong suspicion that she has breast cancer, which is not the field of plastic surgery. So he sent her round to Dr Shun Inamoto in the Mammary Glands Department. There Yūko had an ultrasound, then a biopsy. So they should be able to make a firm diagnosis next week.

Although I had been thinking that her lumps might simply be something like an accumulation of lipid, Dr Nishimura's voice sank, and mine became more high-pitched, as the gravity of her condition became apparent.

Immediately after that, Yūko called me on the phone in an energetic voice, saying she was coming to pick up the car now. Outside the gates, I saw Yūko over there walking towards me. What a tiny wife!

Without letting her know about the telephone conversation I had had with Dr Nishimura, I forced myself to talk cheerfully and asked her how it had all gone. She then told me that the ultrasound had shown a big shadow over her breast, and that the lumps in her armpit appeared to be jet-black on the film. The tone of her voice, however, still made it seem as if she thought this was all no big deal. I wondered how she could possibly be so bright and cheerful, sound so like her normal self. I thought she might have been making herself act cheerfully, but that didn't appear to be the case.

In the afternoon, preoccupied with wondering 'what if…' and imagining the worst case scenario, I couldn't set myself to work…

Today I got home after seven, which was early for me. She is making dinner and waiting for me. Although that's just as usual, I have never felt so grateful. Not even the slightest change from how it always is. However, that it was all the same as always could be considered really special and precious. I wonder why I wasn't aware of that at the time.

The book *Household Medicine* was lying across a chair, open at the information on breast cancer. It's only natural, of course, that she has her doubts. She says that breast cancer is scary, because it can metastasise here and there in the body. I agree, saying that I've heard in many cases this cancer metastatises into the lungs or bones; I talk calmly, as if we are just having a general discussion.

Chatting about the *Tower* journal and so on. After nine o'clock, I invited Yūko to take a walk around the neighbourhood with me. She wasn't too keen, but we took a turn along the Nagatani Shrine and up to the side of Philosopher Shunsuke Tsurumi's house. As we were passing the Nagatani Shrine, I repeated over and over the words 'Please, please, you have to save her.' To rely on the gods for help only at such a time seems rather calculating…

Yūko did not inform me what the two professors had said to her in their consulting room. It was only about a month later that I found out about the situation. At the time, she and our daughter Koh were having serialised in the journal *Kadan* (Tanka Forum), their compositions of more than one tanka a day. From about a year earlier, Yūko and Koh had been having their daily tanka serialised – Yūko's under the umbrella title of *My Tanka Diary*, and Koh's as *Days on the Northern Campus of the University*; it was almost time for this to come to an end.

as 'Mrs Nagata', I was called to room 406; Professor Nishimura

> 'mm, lymph glands
> are hard, aren't they,'
> he says twice,
> then closing the curtains
> goes to the next cubicle

> two doctors were
> looking down at my chest,
> but right away
> they sent my chart round
> to the mammary glands department

in the number two outpatient clinic for mammary surgery, Professor Inamoto Shun was showing me the ultrasound

> images of three
> jet-black lymph glands
> and of mammary glands –
> 'malignant'
> he says, decisively

> right, so it's cancer?
> looking at the ultra-sound
> I think everything
> will be removed, considering
> the spread to my lymph glands

Those were the tanka Yūko recorded for 22 September. How ridiculous was I? Apparently I was the only one thinking she was surprisingly calm; Yūko herself had already been given the verdict 'malignant' by the doctors.

In view of her nerves, I was later on very sorry. I should have requested beforehand that Yūko not be given the diagnosis directly.

'Nothing has been decided yet. There's nothing at all to worry about,' I said, sending her home with an unconcerned expression on my face. But the tanka she composed between the hospital and home are really sad.

I parted from Nagata and drove the car home the usual riverside way

> Kōjin bridge
> Demachiyanagi, Aoi bridge,
> how beautiful these bridges,
> the students too everyone of them –
> in tears I make my way home

> in the little time
> left to me in this world
> what shall I do –
> indigo-coloured Kitayama,
> I must go to you also

The area in Kyoto called Demachiyanagi is a student quarter. Whenever you go there, there are young students and couples strolling around; it's a place overflowing with youthful vitality. We two, also, have met up there and walked around Demachiyanagi, time without number. Yūko must have been seeing lots of students and young people while she was by herself taking the car home. As she was driving along, she was probably overwhelmed with anxiety that she might not be able to view such a scene for long, and so she wept.

For Yūko and for me, Kawabata Street was the very familiar road we took to go just about anywhere. Along it was an avenue of cherry trees, several kilometres in length. In cherry blossom season, it was truly magnificent. And late at night, when the cherry blossoms were falling all at once, it was amazing, a sight that can only be described as 'sublime'. Kawabata Street was probably the road we passed through most. I should probably not have let her go home alone by that route, but I myself was in shock; the truth of the matter was also that I didn't want her to think this was a big deal and worry about it.

Yūko's tanka, placed immediately before the Demachiyanagi one, went like this:

when I was walking along the road beside the hospital, Nagata came from the opposite direction

> how to describe
> the expression on his face
> looking at me –
> I am here,
> not a suspension bridge

This is a poem about me coming to meet Yūko, who was walking towards me from the hospital, on Shōgoin Street. Although I thought that I acted with remarkable sangfroid, my face must have been contorted with emotion or seemed somehow tense. Perhaps I couldn't look straight at Yūko, though she was there right before me. 'I am here, not a suspension bridge.' How pathetic, how painful, those lines. Of all Yūko's tanka, this one is the most bitter for me.

Yūko's operation was performed on 11 October, as day surgery. She was only hospitalised for one night. In the morning, I took Yūko to Kyoto University hospital. She was in the operating theatre before 9 a.m. There was no point in me staying at the hospital, so I went back to my laboratory and worked there through the morning. After midday, a call came from the hospital to say that Yūko's surgery had finished and I should go over there now. I rushed up to the operating theatre on the fifth floor, but Yūko was still groggy; when I spoke to her, she gave some sort of response, but under the effect of the anaesthetic she hardly opened her eyes.

I took advantage of this interval to get an explanation of her condition from the surgeon, Professor Inamoto. He explained that they had set aside what they had taken out, including several lymph glands; having conducted tests during the operation, they had removed what it was possible to remove. Professor Inamoto is well-known for his surgical skill, and I could do nothing but trust in what he said.

The type of surgery performed enabled Yūko to retain her breasts. However, as it had metastasised into her lymph glands, Professor Inamoto considered the cancer to be between stage II and stage III. He added that there was no denying the possibility of further metastasis in the future. It was very difficult for me to realise that fist-sized tissues, which had been part of Yūko, had now been removed and were resting on a surgical tray. It was the strangest feeling, as if samples hitherto used for experiments were being described to me.

About three o'clock, I took Yūko, who had woken from the anaesthetic, and slowly moved her along to a ward. Although she had only just had surgery, she was able to walk to the ward. In the next bed was an elderly lady called Mrs Oyagi, whose surgery had finished a little earlier. On a post-operative high, Mrs Oyagi was chatting on and on in a loud voice to the nurse – so Yūko told me. But Yūko herself was unmistakably on a post-operative high, too, the way she chattered ceaselessly as we walked in the corridor.

When Yūko was in the ward and had settled down a little, Koh came in to take my place by her bedside. I then left for the annual meeting for molecular biology in Yokohama. I couldn't get out of this, as I had been asked to chair the keynote speaker session of the conference. The keynote speech was delivered by the young leader of cell biology studies, Kyoto University Professor Shōichiro Tsukita, who was to die of pancreatic cancer several years after this conference.

I had been asked, some time ago, to perform this role at the conference, and it was simply too difficult to manage to get someone else to substitute for me. The surgery itself had gone well. Yūko understood and accepted the necessity for me to go to Yokohama. In any case, I wanted to make light, as much as possible, of her situation. Nevertheless, I should have stayed with her, at least on the day of her surgery. In subsequent years, Yūko made this absence of mine a major reason to criticise me.

When I reread the tanka I wrote around the time of Yūko's surgery, I myself am dumbfounded at the busy way we stubbornly attempted to continue the same full-on everyday life we had been living up until then. The day before her surgery, on 11 October, Yūko had stayed up until two o'clock in the morning writing work for the journal *NHK Tanka Forum*. On the day of the surgery, I saw her safely through it, then in the evening went off to an academic conference in Yokohama. Three days later, I returned to Kyoto; but the following day I left for a tanka symposium in Kumamoto, so it seemed like I was hardly living at home. It amazes me that, even after then, I continued with an almost unchanged way of life, following, throughout October, a schedule of trips to Tokyo, Nagoya, Marugame, Shiojiri and Kyushu – though admittedly some of these were occasions when I substituted as speaker for Yūko. Leaving at home a sick person who has just had surgery, and going off by myself on business trips, seems a callous thing to do, now I really think about it.

Yūko, too, during this period continued unchangedly composing tanka. Subsequent to the surgery, her shoulder became as hard as a rock, due to the formation of fibrosis, and she was always rubbing her back against a wall. While she massaged herself thus, she was continuing with the serialised poetry for the *Kadan* journal. And then she went up to Tokyo, using a wheelchair, to make an NHK tanka program. Naturally I couldn't tell her to cease such activities.

Perhaps it was both of us stubbornly refusing to give an exaggerated importance to the reality of breast cancer. We didn't want to be defeated by words. We insisted on acting as if we were above consciously grappling with the actual situation of her disease. Then for the first time in a while I read some clinical literature on cancer, and discussed Yūko's case with the doctor in charge of her treatment. We talked about future treatment strategies. I obtained some information on effective treatment methods which were not yet being carried out in Japan, too. I also passed on to Yūko what he told me about the possibility of resurgence of her cancer, and how that could be responded to if it occurred.

From *Soon the Summer Solstice* – Nagata Kazuhiro

About two years after the onset of her illness, Yūko's mental condition became extremely unstable. It was careless of me – and of the family as a whole – that we did not notice her unease and dissatisfaction beginning to build up to depression.

One time – arising completely from a misunderstanding – her deepening depression and resentment erupted and overflowed. It was literally a frenzy of rage. Her anger, once it broke through the dam wall as it were, exploded; and then came an endless flow of bitter words criticising and blaming me.

Yūko's insomnia and her restless sleep were symptomatic even before her illness, but around that time they became even more severe and she was then dependent on tablets of Halcyon, a sleeping drug, for relief. These days there are many doctors who will not prescribe Halcyon, because of its strong side effects on the patient's mental condition. However, at the time not being fully aware of this, Yūko was happy to use Halcyon because of its effectiveness and strength.

Even after taking Halcyon pills and other sedatives, she wouldn't be able to sleep. So she would swallow some more. During that vicious cycle, her mind was becoming clouded. Talking fast and loose, she would start berating me, inarticulately. Always in the same slurred words, abusing me over and over in the same way. That situation went on and on, night after night, without an end in sight. However much I tried to soothe her, tried to reason with her, she would just repeat the same vague expressions, only escalating as she went on.

Sometimes she would take out the kitchen knives, and stick all the household cleavers into the table and the tatami floor. There was no way I could quieten her by myself. Time without number I had to call on Jun or Koh to come to my assistance. Even when Jun or Koh came, she would abuse them in the same way; she would curse us, becoming quite incapable of stopping the violent rush of her words. However we reasoned with her, the more we said, the worse it got – it was like lighting a match to her anger. All we could do was simply not argue at all with her, but persevere in trying to persuade her to go to sleep as soon as possible.

Several times a year there would be particular periods when her condition worsened. They could go on for months. There's an expression 'it was like hell'; and those were truly hell-like times for us, the family now realises. It wasn't just I who suffered; the children's nerves were already in pieces.

Yūko felt I was distancing myself from her illness. That was probably what lay behind the violence of her emotions towards me, I can now rationalise. Of course I understood her unease, but the selfish thinking which filled my mind was that her nervous system could not stand it if I worried excessively about her cancer. I made no changes in my lifestyle hitherto, of going to work at the university, writing articles, and giving lectures.

'Here I am, suffering alone, while my happy-go-lucky husband enjoys himself in his own world. When he comes home, he talks about the pleasant goings-on at his university. I've been home alone all day fighting against anxiety, and he doesn't snuggle up and comfort me,' Yūko must have thought. Those feelings of personal misfortune, and lack of faith in her husband, would have fuelled her doubts and suspicions. I, the most essential person for my wife, was unable to convey properly to Yūko my worries and anxieties. That in itself was a cause of her suffering.

> nothing else for it
> but to act with nonchalance,
> yet
> that nonchalance
> makes her sad
>
> I have tried
> not to lament
> at the same level
> as you – does that
> give you grief, too

> two years have passed
> and my anxieties
> have deepened
> more than yours,
> inexpressibly so
>
> do you blame me
> for the times
> I've wished
> to be the wisest one
> in my little world
>
> sorrowing
> over my failure
> to lament
> along with her,
> she has gone to sleep
>
> Nagata Kazuhiro from The Days After

Those are some of the tanka I wrote around that time. They may seem to be casual compositions, but I was puzzled at her not understanding how I felt. Because I was so very anxious, I hid my concern and acted calm. However, my being superficially patient and tolerant had the reverse effect on Yūko: she felt betrayed by what she saw as my lack of concern. I felt like cursing my inadequacy and immaturity.

I talked it over with the children any number of times. However, there was no technique at all we could employ for solving this problem. Come to the end of all my resources, accompanied by the children, I paid several visits to the psychiatrist, Dr Bin Kimura. I had become acquainted with Dr Kimura during my time as a professor in the Graduate School of Medicine at Kyoto University, under the same professor. I begged him for help.

Dr Kimura examined Yūko at Kyoto Hakuai Hospital. She did not improve immediately, but as three, four, five years were passing, gradually the fierceness and frequency of her explosions lessened. For us family members, it was if there were finally a bright light to illuminate our future.

Although I continued to live in constant fear of Yūko's explosions. I felt things would be okay for us if she could only pass the time in a slightly better mood – even if it meant handling her with kid gloves.

There is not enough space here to touch on all the various happenings, and the feelings of us family members around that period. Meanwhile, eventually, little by little, Yūko seemed to have begun regaining her mental equilibrium.

However – what a blow – just as our family was starting to see a dim light at the end of the tunnel, we were told that Yūko's cancer had reappeared.

16 July 2008

I received a telephone call from Yūko, who had gone to the university hospital to get the results of her regular periodic examination. There were two shadows visible over her liver, so she needed to have a more detailed examination, she told me. The tumour markings, at TPA and NCC – ST 439, were all in excess of the standard values. A thunderbolt. We'd been so confident. It was a full eight years since the cancer surgery. And we'd thought she was fine now.

For the first five years after the surgery, we'd lived secretly counting the years on our fingers. Five years is generally an indicator for the healing of cancers. If the patient gets past the five-year mark, you are presuming she will recover. I was aware that the period before breast cancer can be considered cured is particularly long; nonetheless, once Yūko had got through her five years, we were so excited the five years were over that we opened a bottle of wine to celebrate.

The sixth year passed, the seventh year passed, and then the eighth year was clear. As each year passed, we were overwhelmed with relief that she had pulled through another year. With the eighth year passing, we were on the point of beginning to believe Yūko would be fine.

Her tanka of 16 July:

> unmistakable,
> three sites of metastasis –
> 'has it
> finally come back?' I asked
> my treating physician
>
> Kawano Yūko from *The Reed Boat*

My thought exactly, 'has it finally come back?' Perhaps we had been complacent.

At that time, there were a lot of cheerful happenings around us: the paper produced from my laboratory had been accepted and published in *Science*, a top journal in the life sciences field, and a press release had just been issued. Jun's company Seijisha, which had already published a series of tanka poets, and had received a memorial award for *Wakayama Bokusui*, put out its third publication, *Nagata Kazuhiro*. The plans to rebuild our home, two years in the making, were finalised. We had just moved to another house. As we kept two cats, we could not live in an apartment while our home was being rebuilt, so we moved into what is currently the home of Jun and his family, where we had actually lived earlier. Yūko and I had also just made a start on a series of articles Kyoto Utamakura (Tanka Sites in Kyoto), to be serialised in the *Kyoto* newspaper. As the series was to run over two years, we considered all kinds of locations, and took great pleasure in going around together collecting materials. Then, succeeding me, Yūko was appointed selector for the poems presented to the annual New Year's Poetry Reading at the Imperial Palace.

We had all sorts of nice plans and schedules in place. After clearing eight anxious years, we were almost at the stage of forgetting about Yūko's illness. Maybe we'd become arrogant. Maybe we should have been more modest about the way we spent our time.

Hearing of the reappearance of her cancer, my most immediate worry was that Yūko's mental balance would again become disturbed and unstable. It was certainly very selfish of me, but these were my first thoughts: it had taken us, the family, several years of hard effort to encourage and induce Yūko into maintaining her mental and emotional balance in a steady condition; now there was a real fear that she would once more revert to her earlier state. I should declare, unequivocally, this fear was what immediately assailed me. Rather than pitying poor Yūko, I thought first about myself (I didn't tell her about those first reactions); but of course when I think back now, it is with something like penitence or remorse.

However, this time she was surprisingly composed. Several times she did attack Koh and me with harsh words, but the violence and frenzy, which we'd experienced several years previously, were largely absent. And for that I was extremely grateful.

> just as I am
> sobbing my heart out,
> you come home
> and in silence
> stroke my back

Kawano Yūko from *The Reed Boat*

This time I did not try to bluff it out; and it seemed to give Yūko reassurance that I could grieve with her, or have no hesitation in communicating my sadness to her. Truth to tell, after I knew that her cancer had recurred, I myself was not forced to just stay strong; sometimes, often, I would lay my head on Yūko's knees, or hold her tightly from behind and crying, beg her not to die. While being aware that for me to break down and cry might cause Yūko even more anxiety, I had lost the resilience to be brave, and I wept openly.

Contrarily, my emotional outbursts seemed to make Yūko happier. Saying 'My poor darling,' she rubbed my back endlessly. Probably she felt a certain relief that finally I was worrying at the same level as she was, that I too was deeply concerned – and that we could really experience this whole awful thing together now.

The physician in charge of Yūko's treatment gave her a rough estimate of five years. I had been to talk privately with this doctor, Dr Takeuchi. The doctor had listened to me describe at length my anxieties about the shock and damage to Yūko's nervous system which I feared, before stating that maximum number of years.

Five years did not have a sense of imminence; on the other hand, compared to how long we had already lived, five years was indubitably a short time. There was no doubt that from this period on we could only be conscious of time as a subtraction sum. Inevitably we became aware more than ever of time flying. Subtraction time.

Soon it will be the summer solstice. The winter solstice is something to rejoice about. Realising that the days will rapidly grow lighter from then on, our hearts are brightened even though it is still midwinter. I detest the summer solstice. Thereafter the light days will only grow rapidly shorter.

> each day passing
> subtracts one day
> from the time
> I will have with you –
> soon the summer solstice

>   Nagata Kazuhiro from *The Summer 2010*

It was in July the year before last that it was discovered my wife, Kawano Yūko's, breast cancer had metastasised. Eight years had passed since her surgery, and her family was just starting to feel relieved that all was well. I, whose professional research is connected with cancer, understood full well the implications of metastasis and recurrence without anyone having to spell them out to me.

All at once, my heart filled with the realisation that time now with my wife was of deep and pressing importance. I fervently wished that we could pass each and every day as pleasantly as possible together. Yet, however pleasurable this time, it was still diminishing – which made it even more urgent to cherish what we had left to us.

> how much time
> is remaining for me
> to be with you
> in this house of ours
> answer me, beams!
>
> Kawano Yūko from *The Reed Boat*

Last year we rebuilt our house, and began living in a new house. Although this house had been specifically restructured for our future old age, the time we could now spend together had come to 'how much time is remaining'. Of course my sense of urgency was felt by Yūko as well.

> we never doubted
> that for you
> and for me
> equal time
> would remain
>
> Nagata Kazuhiro from *The Summer 2010*

It had been reasonable to assume I would die first. That seemed obvious as a consequence of my habitually and unreasonably busy and stressful lifestyle. When we spoke of our old age, we always talked up a storm about the prospect of me passing away first. We didn't really think we would have 'equal time'; however, we did anticipate the pleasure of spending another ten years or so growing old together.

I was permeated with the awareness that I was beginning to lose everything that mattered to me. Thus would be the time remaining to me...

It was really hard watching from the sidelines as Yūko suffered through chemotherapy. Even when she was over sixty, Kawano Yūko had amazing black hair, without a single strand of white. The hairstyle she had worn as a younger woman, the shorter hairstyles she adopted as she aged, were all secret sources of pride to her. I loved the nape of her neck. After she had turned fifty, Yūko mostly wore Japanese kimono outfits for her public appearances. When she wore her hair up, in keeping with kimono, her nape-line was extremely beautiful, and I loved it especially.

Immediately before Yūko commenced the anti-cancer drug therapy, the four of us – Koh, Jun, Yūko, and I – went to the Old Imperial Palace in Kyoto to take photographs. Once she had begun chemotherapy, Yūko's hair was bound to start falling out. Before that could happen, I wanted for her to have something left behind which would show the natural glory of her hair. It was more than 'I wanted for her'; for my sake too, I wanted that image of her to remain.

I enticed a rather reluctant Yūko, wearing her favourite pale blue kimono, to accompany us to the Kyoto Imperial Palace to have photographs taken. Ever since the time when he had been a journalist on a fishing magazine, Jun had been virtually a semi-professional camera man. Koh's boyfriend was a professional photographer also; thus, in the spirit of 'learning things without being taught', she applied herself to the photographic tools provided. For a reflector, she had brought along a large piece of cardboard she'd covered with aluminium foil. We took pictures of Yūko with a variety of different types of cameras we had collected: Jun's single lens reflex, Koh's digital camera, and my old Nikon. To the onlookers, this must have been a weird sight.

When I look back on that occasion now, I believe it was a very good thing that we took Yūko out that day and photographed her, even though we had had to force her into it, so to speak. Any photo taken at a nice time will be good, but strangely enough those taken in unfavourable conditions don't come out clearly. On this occasion, we were able to get several lovely, relaxed photos of Yūko looking like her real self. After Yūko died we used all the photos which had been taken that day outside the Kyoto Imperial Palace, first as an enlargement on a panel two metres wide by three metres high, on the central altar at her commemorative service, then for the cover of the book *Kawano Yūko* published by Seijisha, and also for the wrapping band of this book.

Parents and children, the four of us strolled around the Imperial Palace with the same thought: for each of three of us to take photos of the one person. It is sad, but whenever we recall that day, our memories are clouded with nostalgia. If we hadn't had the photographs of that occasion, we her family would not have been able to fix in our collective memory the image of Yūko wearing such lovely expressions. Yūko herself was thoroughly delighted the photos had been taken. It was more than a matter of just leaving nice pictures behind; what gave her so much joy, probably, was that the photography session had been a joint family enterprise.

The year 2010. To review the efficacy of the chemotherapy, she was finally admitted to Kyoto University Hospital in June. And then discharged on 7 July, the day of the Tanabata Star Festival. There were no more anti-cancer drugs Yūko could be given. If further chemotherapy was administered, it would endanger her life, which was already teetering on the brink, we were informed. All that was left now was palliative care.

Sometime earlier, preparations had been set in place for Yūko to enter a terminal care ward. Yūko too accepted and understood this, and we had been to check it out. However, when things got to that stage, Yūko expressed her wish to spend the remaining time in her own home. As her loving family we could hardly object to this.

Whatever marvellous facilities are arrayed there, whatever pleasant spaces have been provided, a hospital is still a hospital. Even if family members kept her company in the hospital twenty-four hours a day, it could not be the same as an everyday living environment. A hospital is place one goes to in the consciousness of going; it's a place where one stays in the consciousness of staying for the sake of giving care. One's relationship with the patient, also, inevitably becomes a matter of one-on-one. I myself wanted more than anything to spend Yūko's last days with her 'amid everyday life'. We would continue our normal lives, and Yūko would be there too, albeit bedridden; that was where and how we wanted her, nestled beside us.

In the final analysis, I believe it was the right choice to have made. Kawano Yūko literally kept on composing tanka until her final day. The tanka which she left written in a notebook in faintly pencilled letters, numbered close to two hundred, all composed in the month or so before her death. Lying in bed she continued writing tanka on anything which was to hand. Tissue boxes, pill bags, anything at all.

And then, gradually she became too weak to hold a pencil. When she got to that stage, she would, without warning, mutter out the words of a new poem as if conversing. In a flurry, whoever of us happened to be with her at the time would take down her words. That was how it went – Koh or Jun or I would write out and copy Yūko's tanka for her.

11th August

Yūko's condition worsened, little by little. From the day before, she had been extremely nauseous. The patch from which morphine was continuously soaking into her skin was taken off. Possibly as a result of that, she was scratching her chest in agony from the morning onwards. She told me it was hurting her unbearably to breathe. I changed her position. But there was no change in her pain. Covered in sweat, she went from saying 'I'm in such pain, do something' to 'Let me die, now.'

She asked me to take the thin oxygen tubes out of her nose. She said her nightdress was hurting her, so I cut it open with scissors. Each time she verbalised her pain she needed more oxygen, and in turn her breathing became laboured. I could do nothing but hold her hand and repeat over and over, 'It's all right, it's all right,' while cursing to myself my own powerlessness. 'Don't try to talk any more, just take slow breaths,' I said, stroking her head.

Her hair, which had all fallen out at one stage, had eventually grown back to about a centimetre in length. There was not a single white hair among the black. Stroking it felt like stroking a baby's soft hair. The very softness of her hair was pitiful.

Koh suddenly began talking about our life in America. And I, understanding what she intended, immediately responded to this.

The fun we had on the way when we took Jun and Koh to their respective summer camps some three hundred kilometres distant. 'Yūko, do you remember?' I'd say in between reminiscences, as the two of us talked desperately of our time in America, recalling one thing after another. The topic of conversation flowed across Yūko's agonised countenance, slowly unfolding; then finally the morphine emission began to take effect and she fell asleep.

Perhaps, hopefully, she was cradled in her sleep by those happy recollections of our time as a young family. Soon she would sleep the sleep of the dead. We prayed that on the verge of the final sleep, her mind would continue to be filled with memories of our happy times together. Because those memories were our family itself.

After she had slept for about an hour, she woke and seemed to notice us watching her from both sides of the bed. She looked at me very strangely, and in a sort of mutter, slowly, barely audibly, began speaking in a tiny voice, saying, 'All of you, your feelings, so much...'

Ah, I thought. Saying 'Just a moment,' I opened a piece of manuscript paper. It was a poem. 'Though I understand so well,' I wrote hurriedly in pencil. After a few minutes, 'How few words there are to leave with you now.' Written out in tanka form, this was:

> though I understand
> so well, the feelings
> of you all,
> how few words there are
> to leave with you now

When she had composed a tanka in her mind, the words would come out one after another, like sweet potatoes on a vine. During the next ten minutes, Yūko composed several tanka.

The final poem Yūko composed was this:

> reaching out my hand
> I want to touch you all,
> my dear ones – but
> I haven't enough breath left
> not in this world

And thus, Kawano Yūko was composing tanka until the day she died. She was a born poet, I believe.

The next day, 12 August. Immediately after a spasm of pain, it seemed, she muttered, 'I won't forget.'

'And next comes...' I said, encouraging her.

'Mm, that's enough,' she responded.

That was the moment when poet Kawano Yūko left her poetry.

*

After Yūko's death, we family members carried out the task of collecting the tanka which she had left behind, not just on pieces of manuscript paper, but also in notebooks and on medicine bags and so on. While putting together word after word what Yūko had written in her notebooks, as she continued to compose tanka right up until her death, we her family could feel the trust she had placed in us.

The very fact she had faith that if she wrote things down, some member of her family would collect her words and make them public as tanka – even if they had to be dictated while she was suffering from the after-effects of chemotherapy, and had oxygen tubes attached to her, meant she was able to be certain of leaving her legacy of these tanka. She must have thought it was a very reassuring and happy thing that there were three other poets in our family.

While I was copying out by hand those tanka of Yūko's, deciphering her writing and decoding their meaning, I could not help but be subconsciously overwhelmed by feelings of reverence. Here was a poet who had genuinely loved tanka, who had been born to compose tanka. Even if she was unable to see them in print with her own eyes, they were tanka which she had kept on composing as naturally as she breathed. In the purity of her devotion to the continuing task of composing tanka, I believe that Kawano Yūko was a true poet, born and bred. She was also my wife. I am so proud of that.

> 'good morning'
> we awoke and gathered
> around you
> who would never
> open her eyes again

you, the only you,
are missing
on an autumn day
when the light of this world
shines on the cosmos flowers

'idiot,' you say laughing
with your head thrown back –
again you laugh,
but you are not there
in your chair

'deceased wife,'
how can I
refer to you like that?
my palms remember
your palms

shall we have a drink
I'd say, when there was
someone to respond,
when we had time together
just the two of us

am I a sissy?
that's too bad –
I simply cannot
shut you away
under the stone

Nagata Kazuhiro from *Elegies*

Afterword

Recently I wrote the following tanka:

> I must not die,
> for when I die
> you will
> really
> be dead

The deceased can only live in the memories of the living. Therefore I, who knew Kawano Yūko best of all, want to go on living for a long time. That is the only way of keeping her alive.

On the other hand, however, Kawano Yūko will be remembered in certain places other than in my own recollections. It goes without saying, she will live on in her collected works. And her many, many, readers will keep their own versions of Kawano Yūko in their hearts and memories…

Nagata Kazuhiro

Appendix

Book-length translations and co-translations of Kawano Yūko's work by Amelia Fielden MA:

Time Passes (Saigetsu) 1995, tanka collection of Kawano Yūko's work; complete translation submitted to the University of Canberra and awarded Postgraduate Diploma in Languages in 2000

Time Passes (Saigetsu) 1995, tanka collection; bilingual; abridged in the book *Fountains Play and Times Passes*; Ginninderra Press, 2002

Vital Forces (Tairyoku), 1998 tanka collection; bilingual; co-translated with Yuhki Aya; Bookpark, Nagoya, Japan, 2004

As Things Are, anthology, 100 tanka selected by Manaka Tomohisa from 10 collections by Kawano Yūko; Ginninderra Press, 2005

My Tanka Diary (Hizuke no Aru Uta), 2002 prose plus poetry diary by Kawano Yūko; complete annotated translation in two volumes; submitted to the University of Newcastle and awarded the degree of Master of Arts in 2005

My Tanka Diary (Hizuke no Aru Uta); abridged version, Ginninderra Press, 2006

The Time of This World, anthology, 100 tanka selected by Ōshima Shiyo from thirteen collections by Kawano Yūko; Modern English Tanka Press, Baltimore, Maryland, USA, 2010

The Maternal Line (Bōkei), 2008 tanka collection; co-translated with Ogi Saeko; Modern English Tanka Press, Baltimore, Maryland, USA, 2011

For Instance, Sweetheart (Tatoeba Kimi): Forty Years of Love Songs; autobiographical essays and tanka poetry by Kawano Yūko and her husband, Nagata Kazuhiro; Ginninderra Press, 2017

Amelia has also had published sixteen books of her translations of tanka written by various other poets.

www.ingramcontent.com/pod-product-compliance
Lightning Source LLC
Chambersburg PA
CBHW030907080526
44589CB00010B/187